Six Steps in the Treatment of Borderline Personality Organization

Six Steps in the Treatment of Borderline Personality Organization

Vamık D. Volkan, M.D.

Jason Aronson Inc.
Northvale, New Jersey
London

10 9 8 7 6 5 4 3 2 1

Library of Congress Cataloging-in-Publication Data

Volkan, Vamık D., 1932–
Six steps in the treatment of borderline personality organization.
Bibliography: p.
Includes index.
1. Borderline personality disorder—Case studies.
2. Psychotherapy—Case Studies. 3. Transference (Psychology)—Case studies. I. Title. [DNLM:
1. Personality disorders—therapy. 2. Transference (Psychology). WM 190 V916s]
RC569.5.B67V65 1987 616.89 87-19475
ISBN 0-87668-753-2

Manufactured in the United States of America.

To L. Bryce Boyer,
for encouraging me to continue working
with undeveloped and severely regressed patients,
and for his friendship.

Contents

Acknowledgments

The Charlottesville Study Group for Psychoanalytic Psychotherapy, made up of former psychiatric residents at the University of Virginia, met for six years starting in 1974. They discussed weekly with me material from their work with patients, providing a most useful arena for learning, teaching, and exploring. My thoughts about the six steps in the treatment of psychosis-prone borderline patients began to take form in my sessions with these bright young professionals.

My first formal presentation of this topic was made at a symposium called "Dialogues on Borderlines," held at the Institute of the Pennsylvania Hospital in Philadelphia on April 3–4, 1981. Since then I have made presentations on the subject at various psychiatric centers and medical schools in the United States, Mexico, Germany, and Finland, receiving valuable comments from many colleagues. So I express here my gratitude to the Charlottesville Study Group and the colleagues who offered useful suggestions at my presentations.

I also thank Antti Kumento, M.D., of Turku, Finland, for sharing with me his observations on the psychoanalytic treatment of a severely regressed patient, and I owe a debt of gratitude to Gregory Saathoff, M.D., of Charlottesville, Virginia, for allowing me to include material from his work.

Lastly, I would like to express my gratitude to Mrs. Virginia Kennan, my friend and editorial assistant for two decades, for editing this book and providing for me an intellectual sounding board as my writing progressed.

Six Steps in the Treatment of Borderline Personality Organization

Introduction

This book deals with the *technique* used in treating psychosis-prone borderline patients. I perceive borderline personality organization on a spectrum, at the lower end of which are undeveloped and/or severely regressed patients prone to psychotic experiences and focalized and temporary psychotic transferences. I focus on the therapeutic regression and subsequent progressive developments that occur over the course of lengthy and intense treatment in which the patient successfully identifies with some of the therapist's functions, particularly his ability to analyze and integrate. There is always the danger with already severely regressed or undeveloped individuals that regression during therapy will cause further disorganization and increase expression of that primitive and pregenital aggression so very disturbing in treatment. Thus, techniques that make the process useful while avoiding this unfavorable outcome are emphasized. Focalized transference psychosis can be confined to the consultation room.

The entire treatment is set forth in six steps, which are not artificially selected. They reflect the patients' actual sequential experiences in the therapeutic process. My treatment method is psychoanalytic; the ways in which I modify it from psychoanalysis proper as applied to patients who are neurotic and of a higher level of personality organization will become evident when described in detail.

The six steps are as follows:

1. The Establishment of a Reality Base

The first step covers the time between the diagnostic interviews and the establishment of the core of a therapeutic alliance. These very disturbed patients cannot be expected to accomplish a therapeutic alliance in the true sense, so we must look for its nucleus—the core that depends upon the patient's recognizing the analyst's own confidence in his technique and his underlying and unspoken commitment to the patient's well-being. The patient senses that the analyst is different from his disturbing internalized object representations. At some point in this first phase, the patient will be asked to use the couch.

2. The First Split Transference

The second step involves settling down on the couch and includes a period of relating "chaotically" to the analyst, just as the patient relates to life in general. Manifestations of *defensive* splitting and related primitive defense mechanisms color the sessions at this time. At a crucial juncture, the patient's opposite self- and object units meet, signaling the conclusion of this step.

3. Focalized Psychotic Transference Leading to Reactivated and Transference-Related Transitional Phenomena

In this phase we see therapeutic regression in which focalized transference psychosis and corresponding counterresponse appear. The patient uses newly activated transitional phenomena to progress away from this regressive state.

4. The Second Split Transference

Developmental splitting that leads to the mending of opposing self- and object representations appears in transference here.

5. The Development of Transference Neurosis

A transference neurosis develops, and vicissitudes of the Oedipus complex become evident, genuine in the sense that they are experienced with mended self- and object representations for the first time. The mechanism of repression replaces primitive splitting to a great extent.

6. The Third Split Transference and Termination

The last step deals with termination issues. The patient usually reviews, overhauls, and resolves conflicts in his object relations as they are reactivated by knowledge of the impending separation and are unrepressed.

The first two steps concern the time during which the patient is being prepared for therapeutic regression. The third step concerns the therapeutic regression itself; the next two deal with progressive development, and the final step with termination.

I derive my data from work with nine psychosis-prone borderline patients who underwent the specific treatment that I describe in this book and whom I saw for an average of six years, four times a week. While the number of patients is relatively small, the intensity and the length of my involvement with each one of them provided valuable data, data that I believe could not have been obtained by other methods. Furthermore, I have amplified the observations I derived from my work with them through my extensive experience with other types of severely regressed or undeveloped patients and high-level borderline individuals, and through experience supervising other therapists treating similar patients.

Dividing this book into two parts, I begin by describing the metapsychology of borderline personality organization in general, reviewing the prevailing attitudes toward borderline patients before turning to my own work with patients prone to psychosis.

In Chapter 3 I shift the focus to the psychology of the analyst or therapist who treats such patients and stress the importance of proper training. The last two chapters of Part I deal with technical issues and explain why therapeutic regression as an antecedent to progressive development may be preferable as a way of dealing with psychosis-prone individuals. I hold that these patients will have maximum structural change and progression if their therapy permits therapeutic regression.

Anyone studying the techniques of a treatment method should be supervised at each stage of the treatment. The activation of conflicts, the patient's identification with functions of the therapist, transference and countertransference manifestations, and other processes vary according to phases of the treatment. It is no wonder that the American Psychoanalytic Association's affiliated psychoanalytic institutes require each candidate to have not only the required number of hours of supervision but supervision at every stage of the analysis, including the termination phase. Accordingly, I believe that anyone seeking to teach or share his technique, beyond supervising a few individuals, should be able to document his competence by describing the *total* treatment of at least one patient. Although case vignettes are helpful, they do not tell the entire story.

Part II of this book describes the case of a psychosis-prone borderline individual and serves to illustrate the six steps of treatment and how I think and feel while working with a patient.

PART I

Chapter 1

Clinical Observations and Theoretical Considerations

BORDERLINE PERSONALITY ORGANIZATION

Because the subjects in this book are mainly "psychosis-prone" (Gunderson et al. 1975, Boyer 1986) borderline patients, it would be well to discuss at the outset what is meant by *borderline personality organization*. The term has had considerable attention in the literature of psychoanalysis and psychiatry since the late 1960s. Here I limit discussion to the ways in which this type of psychic organization appeared in the background of the patients whose treatment I report.

Classification by Structural Configuration

Kernberg (1967, 1975) holds that the borderline patient has a *specific* and pathological personality organization, and suggests that this diagnosis be arrived at according to the structural configuration of a patient rather than according to his symptoms and personality traits, even when the latter are highly suggestive. He classifies patients according to the two tasks of the early ego: to differentiate self- and object representations, and to integrate the differentiated self- and object representations. These are initially polarized, influenced either by libidinal drive derivatives, in which case they are "good," or by aggressive ones, in which case they are "bad" (Jacobson 1964). Neurotics, or those with an advanced level of ego organization, have accomplished both of these tasks; psychotic patients have accomplished neither.

Kernberg notes that patients with borderline personality organization are those who have accomplished the first, but not the second, of these tasks and thus cannot synthesize opposing self- and object images or representations and the affective states associated with them. Especially important is his explanation that this lack of integrative capacity is used defensively by the ego of the patient with borderline personality organization. He calls this *defense splitting* and considers it the dominant defense of such patients. Splitting occurs naturally in the course of an individual's development; the infant cannot at first mend (integrate) those self- and object images having libidinal drive investment with those having aggressive drive investment. This developmental splitting disappears as the ego of the child slowly develops integrative functions. Most observers suggest that mending begins at about 6 months of age and is completed, for all practical purposes, around 36 months of age. Kernberg emphasizes that when something interferes with the integrative ability, splitting continues, but it now becomes a defense mechanism. Other defenses often used by persons with borderline personality organization—such as primitive idealization, primitive forms of projection, denial, devaluation, and omnipotence—are centered around splitting. Thus the ego is protected from object relations conflict "by means of dissociating or actively keeping apart contradictory experiences of the self and of significant others. These contradictory ego states are alternately activated, and, as long as they can be kept separate from each other, anxiety related to these conflicts is prevented or controlled" (Kernberg 1980, p. 6).

One of my patients illustrated in a clinical setting the way in which contradictory experiences are kept separate.

> Many months into his treatment he began coming to his sessions 25 minutes late. He was seeing me four times a week and using the couch. I tolerated his tardiness for nearly a month before confronting him with it. It then became clear that he did arrive at my office building on time, but upon arrival went into the lavatory adjoining my office, where for 25 minutes he created in his mind a "bad" image of me and a corresponding "bad" one of himself to interact with it. Then he would make his way to my office, where the door always stood open for him and where I sat waiting. Lying on the couch, he would smile in a reflection of his good image and induce a pleasant sensation in me that reflected a good image of me. Then he would start the session—or what was left of it—by saying, " . . . and another thing, Dr. Volkan!" as though one "good" session were the continuation of another. His opposing experiences with me, as well as his own opposing self-image, all of which had been the subject of rumination in the lavatory, were altogether apart from the pleasurable experience taking place in my office.

Although this vignette exemplifies the way splitting appears in a clinical setting, we must remember that the splitting of self- and object images does not occur automatically, but that each of the images involved in this process has its own developmental history and is connected with affective states and infantile pathogenic fantasies. The patient who activated images of himself and me in the lavatory had been greatly overprotected in childhood by his mother. She had given him frequent enemas from the time of his early infancy, not for constipation but as a way of allaying her anxiety over perfect cleanliness, and he had been unable to integrate the image of a devoted mother with that of one so physically intrusive. It is not surprising that while being treated by me he showed marked splitting.

Classification by Ego Defenses

Classification of patients may also take into consideration the use of ego defenses. Kernberg is very specific about separating high- and low-level defense constellations. Neurotics, or those with high-level defense operations—such as reaction formation and rationalization—center around the dominant mechanism of repression. Those with borderline personality organization use low-level defenses such as primitive projections and denial, all of which center around splitting.

Psychotics also use primitive defense mechanisms, but, according to Kernberg, they do so mainly to protect themselves from further disintegration of the boundaries between self and object; then the potential for fusing the self-experience with the experience of important others is reduced. Volkan and Akhtar (1979) describe how splitting as a defense is not crystallized in the schizophrenic, and how other primitive defenses such as the projection of self- and object representations (externalization) do not provide lasting comfort, because schizophrenics can *identify* themselves with whatever they have externalized more readily than can borderline patients. *Projective identification*, as this process is usually called in psychoanalytic writings, is a rather stable defense in those with borderline personality organization who maintain obligatory contact with the object into which they project their intrapsychic experiences, and then try to control it as though to keep from having to take back what has been projected. They empathize with and identify to some degree with the object. Quick identification dominates in schizophrenia; what is projected is soon felt within the subject, and this precludes taking any lasting comfort from the maneuver. The thrusting out and externalization of unwanted units, and their subsequent replacement within, differs from one patient to another and prevails among schizophrenics without providing significant comfort. It gives borderline patients a more stable defense against anxiety. This process may result in fusion, defusion, and refusion of self- and object images or representations. According to Kernberg, such states are typical in schizophrenia, but they appear only briefly and temporarily in patients with borderline personality organization. Kernberg makes a clear distinction between the borderline and the psychotic individual.

Volkan and Akhtar (1979) see defensive qualities, however extremely primitive, in fusion, defusion, and refusion. Some fusion relates to very primitive pathogenic fantasies that are libidinally determined. The patient "consumes" the representation of a good object in order to experience ecstatic union, but in patients like schizophrenics, any good object, whether fused with the subject or not, can quickly turn into a bad one.

Paradoxically, most fusions in schizophrenia seem to interrelate with aggressive fantasies. The patient "kills" a terrifying object image by fusing with it—consuming it—but then he feels terror within because of the fusion that has taken place. No satisfactory solution is achieved; externalization of the terrifying unit follows, and the patient seems to be arrested in a fusion or defusion cycle and to be using very primitive defenses against object relations conflict.

Ego Weakness

Kernberg also describes patients with borderline structure from the standpoint of ego psychology, speaking of the *relative* strength as well as the weakness of their egos. Such patients are relatively intact in reality testing and thought processes. Because of their relatively sound adaptation to reality and interpersonal relations, they may seem fairly normal, but it should be remembered that their state is only relatively normal and may, as I will show later, give way to brief psychotic moments in regression. Kernberg emphasizes, however, that such patients tend to maintain their relative strength over time, and because of their comparatively sound capacity for reality testing and interpersonal relations, borderline patients should not be confused with the truly psychotic.

Ego weakness in the individual with borderline personality organization includes poor tolerance of frustration, poor impulse control, and proclivity to use primitive ego defenses and identity diffusion.

Identity Diffusion

Kernberg uses Erikson's term (1950, 1956) *identity diffusion* (see Akhtar 1984, for a concise review of this syndrome) to describe the basic problem of the patient with borderline personality organization—the absence of an integrated self-concept and an integrated concept of others. This shortcoming is reflected in a chronic subjective feeling of emptiness, a shallow and contradictory perception of oneself and others, and an inability to integrate emotionally behavior patterns that are contradictory.

Pregenital Aggression

Kernberg holds that the ego's second task—to integrate self- and object representations formed under the influence of libidinal drive derivatives and their related affects with the corresponding self- and object representations—is not accomplished because of a pathological predominance of pregenital aggression, especially oral aggression. Such aggression "tends to induce premature development of oedipal strivings, and as a consequence a particular pathological condensation between pregenital and genital aims under the overriding influence of aggressive needs" (Kernberg 1967, p. 681).

In indicating why some people develop a borderline personality organization, then, Kernberg points to a failure to develop and complete the integration of opposing representations of self as well as opposing representations of their respective corresponding affective states.

Abend, Porder, and Willick

Abend and colleagues (1983) provide a thoughtful review of the concept of borderline personality, as well as a study of Kernberg's formulations. Their monograph is based on the work of the Kris Study Group of the New York Psychoanalytic Institute, on extended discussions of four analyzed patients diagnosed as being borderline, and on a lengthy exchange with Kernberg. In reviewing the literature, these writers found substantial agreement among various descriptions of borderline cases. Nonetheless, they remain dissatisfied with the accuracy of the term *borderline* to indicate a specific diagnostic category and see variables in respect to specific individual characteristics. Thus they prefer to diagnose each case according to the patient's specific psychic structure, using such terms as *severe sadomasochistic character disorder*. They disagree, then, with Kernberg's belief that all who have a borderline personality organization share such features as similar internalized object relations, similar dominant defenses, or similar ego structures.

Basing their findings primarily on observation of the four analyzed patients discussed at Kris Study Group meetings, Abend and colleagues suggest that oedipal-phase conflicts play an important role in the object relations of these cases, and that profound identification with disturbed parents contributed significantly to the personality development of the patients under study and helped determine their character traits, thought processes, and symptom formation. Stating that oedipal-phase conflict is often neglected or minimized in the literature dealing with the development of borderline psychopathology—including Kernberg's contribution—they were impressed by the influence of oedipal-level conflicts in the pathological features of the four cases studied. These cases exhibited preoedipal conflicts as well, but they "could not specify that the crucial etiological determinants for the development of all borderline patients took place between the ages of 8 months to 18 months" (p. 107). They do not, therefore, subscribe to the idea that the main etiological factor is preoedipal fixation. Regression from oedipal-level issues seems to them a more acceptable explanation, one at least as important as preoedipal factors.

Finally, Abend and colleagues disagree with Kernberg in respect to the defensive constellations of these patients. They feel that defenses in general should not be described as either primitive or advanced, and that any defense should be evaluated according to the total ego organization of each patient. Borderline patients, they suggest, use all kinds of defense mechanisms including repression. Although they agree that a toddler may "split" the mental representation of the mother into all-good and all-bad segments and displace all-bad feelings onto another object in order to preserve the good relationship with his mother, they believe "that such 'splitting' does not represent an immutable fixation which persists unchanged into adult mental life" (p. 165).

OBJECT RELATIONS THEORIES

Kernberg (1976a) described at least three types of object relations theory. The first broadly concerns the understanding of present interpersonal relations in terms of past ones (something that applies to virtually all psychoanalytic approaches, in which we examine the mental structures that preserve past interpersonal experiences and the relationship between such structures) and derivatives of instinctual needs in the psychosocial environment.

The second theory, at the opposite extreme, is based on the concepts of Melanie Klein and W. R. D. Fairbairn. The third theory is one that Kernberg himself endorses, acknowledging his debt to such theoreticians as Edith Jacobson, Margaret Mahler, and Erik Erikson. His theory of object relations assumes that

> . . . the earliest internalization processes have dyadic features, that is, a self-object polarity, even when self- and object representations are not yet differentiated. By the same token, all future developmental steps also imply dyadic internalizations, that is, internalization not only of an object as an object representation, but of an interaction of the self with the object, which is why I consider units of self- and object representations (and the affect dispositions linking them) the basic building blocks on which further developments of internalized object and self-representations, and later on, the overall tripartite structure (ego, superego, and id) rest. [Kernberg 1980, p. 17]

The object relations theory described by Kernberg is not an additional metapsychological insight but, rather, an integral part of ego psychology. Kernberg (1984) states that "internalized object relations constitute substructures of the ego, substructures that are, in turn, hierarchically organized" (p. 5). I have examined the relationship between this object relations theory and the overall structural theory (Volkan 1981a), pointing out the close relationship between the maturing ego and the establishment and differentiation of self- and object representations. This relationship is not unlike the reciprocal benefit that plants receive from the very soil they are sown to enrich. As object representations are successfully formed and some of them are assimilated into self-representations by means of identification, the ego gleans enough nourishment to continue to differentiate from id, and, in turn, to further yield mature object relations.

I have stated (1981a) that structural theory is still the best instrument for understanding the psychopathology of patients with fully differentiated id, ego, and superego, and for success in handling transference–countertransference manifestations in their treatment. I agreed that this theory is not, however, very useful when applied to the treatment of patients whose dominant psychopathology reflects the reactivation of primitive internalized object relations. I went on to indicate, as I had previously noted (Volkan 1976) that once a patient in treatment resolves the psychopathology that reflects his reactivation of primitive internalized object relations, he moves on to exhibit conflicts best understood and interpreted with the use of structural theory. In a sense I saw a hierarchical model in the process of understanding a patient's psychic experiences as he matures. This idea parallels Gedo and Goldberg's argument (1973) for limiting consideration of the tripartite model to psychopathology exhibited at a higher developmental level.

SPLITTING AND AMBIVALENCE

In 1976 I observed that when patients with borderline personality organization commence treatment they exhibit a dominant reactivation of their primitive internalized object relations and in doing so use splitting as described by Kernberg. Abend and colleagues (1983) imply that there is no difference between intense ambivalence and splitting, but I hold that there is a difference that can be understood by examining the ego's integrative function. The sicker the borderline patient is, the more his "ambivalence" corresponds to Kernberg's definition of splitting. Buie (1985), in reviewing the book by Abend and colleagues (1983), concludes that they studied only four patients healthy enough for classical analysis. Moreover, certain clinical phenomena are imprecisely classified when the concept of ambivalence is used and are better understood with the concept of splitting. Dorpat (1976) endorses Buie's assertions, referring to Burnham's "object need-fear dilemma" (1969) as an example. A schizophrenic has a need for and a fear of support from others. His excessive need for objects makes him fearful since these objects can destroy him through abandonment. Objects can make or break such a patient. They are either all needed (good) or all rejecting (bad). Dorpat suggests that this clinical phenomenon cannot be described by the concept of ambivalence.

I believe the concept of ambivalence also cannot explain the "little man phenomenon" (Kramer 1955, Niederland 1956, Volkan 1965); however, the concept of splitting is highly informative here. The "little man phenomenon" explains how an unintegrated self-representation (the little man) remains separate from the rest of the self-representation. I suggest, contrary to the conclusions of Abend and colleagues, that splitting can remain unchanged into adult life. I believe this is so because in my work with borderline or severely regressed patients, these patients exhibited their splitting behavior in such a way that it dominated the transference phenomenon. More importantly, at one point in their treatment they mended their split psychic experiences after identifying with the analyst's integrating functions and after enriching their egos. I have given clinical examples of this elsewhere (Volkan 1975, 1976, 1982a), and I give further examples in my description of Pattie's progress in Part II of this book.

Buie (1985) also maintains that the borderline patient develops ambivalence *in* treatment. This development of true ambivalence occasions great distress and anxiety, with guilt and turning of hate onto the self, often with suicidal intent. My findings support Buie's observations, but I must add that the better the patient is prepared therapeutically for the occasion of mending, the more a process like mourning, though with less guilt, replaces a process like depression, with guilt, at the time of mending.

DEVELOPMENTAL SPLITTING

I agree with others (e.g., Berg 1977) that mending of the *developmental* splitting is never totally accomplished (Volkan 1981a), although, as I have stated, we expect a child whose developmental course is uncomplicated to complete the mending process *for all practical purposes* by the age of 36 months. What happens to the unmended good and bad self-representations? Kernberg himself (1976b) answered this question, suggesting after van der Waals (1952) that with the newly developed—or more precisely, increased—repression some unintegrated representations are pushed into the id, making that portion of it an "ego id."

Integration of opposing representational units brings about a feeling of loss; when this happens to a patient in a clinical setting he experiences a sense of mourning. The child reacts to the "loss" of his good units by establishing a new set of representations. These are idealized as unmended good units, but are not, like his good units, absolutely good, being more closely connected with realistic aspects of objects and the self. In turn, these idealized images coalesce through identifications into superego identifications. Since the precursors of the superego contain some unmended and excessively bad images, the new images help tame the ferocity of the superego.

The Child's Externalizations

In examining what happens to our unintegrated self- and object images, I have suggested (Volkan 1985a, 1985b, 1986) the presence of a phenomenon with cultural, social, and political implications, and have offered the view that under the influence of mothering persons, the child deposits, through externalization, some of his unmended self- and object representations and their accompanying feeling states into certain reservoirs in the environment. I call these reservoirs, which are stable, "suitable targets of externalization." Familiar aspects of the child's home or neighborhood, that is, the ethnic soup or other possessions indicative of bonding that Mack (1984) calls "cultural amplifiers," become targets upon which the child externalizes his unmended aspects of himself for "safekeeping." There are reservoirs for good unmended aspects as well as for bad ones. When these reservoirs are stable, they can contain the child's externalizations for a long period of time, perhaps even a lifetime, in order to help him to keep more integrated self- and object representations within himself and to avoid object relations conflicts. The suitable targets of externalization sponsored for children by the important others in their group (i.e., ethnic, national) who share identical investment in them, make the children alike inasmuch as all draw from the same reservoir. I have noted elsewhere how such inanimate shared reservoirs might be the psychological beginnings of concepts of an ethnic or nationalistic group's enemies (bad suitable targets of externalization) and allies (good suitable targets of externalization) in the social and political sense.

Children externalize their unmended bad self- and object units in accordance with the pleasure principle, since it helps them retain the mended (realistic) as well as good and idealized representations of important others. But we must ask why children also externalize their good unmended self- and object images, and why they may share a reservoir to contain such good units for such a long period of time, indeed, throughout life. Why, for example, do Finnish children invest the sauna with such good units and with higher symbolic meanings (Tähkä et al. 1971)?

It seems that the inevitable frustrations a child experiences may load the representation of his experiences, especially the representations of people involved in them, with the derivatives of the aggressive drive. In a sense, the child does not want to experience contamination of some of his good units by his aggressive ones and may seek to protect them. Under the direction of important others, his real experiences make him "think" that certain things "out there"—the ethnic soup, the sauna—can absorb and protect his good units. Such good, inanimate, suitable targets seem always to contain aspects of a good mother.

I have described only briefly my ideas on suitable targets of externalization (for an elaboration see Volkan 1985a, 1985b, 1986). I emphasize here that splitting, in an unchanged as well as a changed manner, finds expression in adult life, and that we all make use of it; it is not limited to the borderline individual. For example, we are likely to think in terms of black and white when in reality, expressions of our own ethnicity, nationality, and so on, should in all fairness be compared with those exhibited by a common enemy, and be seen as competing. Disregard for the realities of the other side is considered normal if sanctioned by one's own ethnic or national group.

DEFENSIVE SPLITTING

The difference between neurotic patients and those with a high-level ego organization is apparent insomuch as splitting is used as a defense mechanism. I agree with Abend and colleagues (1983) that borderline patients, even schizophrenics, "use a good deal of repression, even though in acute regressive states formerly repressed instinctual drive derivatives may emerge." They also state, "We found repression operating along with other defenses in our patients" (p. 155). In many, perhaps all, patients we see the simultaneous operation of splitting and related mechanisms, and repression and related mechanisms. In 1984 I described the entire analysis of a patient who, in addition to utilizing sophisticated defense mechanisms, used splitting; splitting was particularly marked whenever he regressed therapeutically. This patient, however, was not considered to be borderline, although he had borderline characteristics among his many neurotic psychopathological and higher-level (obsessional) personality traits.

Object Relations versus Structural Conflict

Patients with borderline personality organization tend to use splitting and related mechanisms when there is urgent conflict, particularly when it is an object relations conflict and not structural. They use repression and related mechanisms when the conflict is not urgent, especially if it is a structural conflict.

Dorpat (1976) offers a way of differentiating object relations conflict from structural; he holds that the general application of the tripartite (id–ego–superego) structural model to all developmental levels tends to obliterate important differences among psychopathologies at various developmental levels. Dorpat assumes that not all psychic conflict is of the type that involves the tripartite structure. Object relations conflicts involve a less differentiated psychic structural antecedent to an advanced id–ego–superego differentiation. Describing what he considers *the crucial difference* between structural conflict and the conflict of object relations, he says

> . . . in a structural conflict, the subject experiences (or is capable of experiencing if some part of the conflict is uncon-

> scious) the opposing tendencies as aspects of himself. . . . In the object relations conflict, the subject experiences the conflict as being between his own wishes and his representations (e.g., introjects) of another person's values, prohibitions, or injunctions. [pp. 869–870]

He adds that conflicts concerning dependency and independence, and closeness to and distance from objects, are little understood without the concept of object relations.

Splitting and Repression in the Borderline Individual

Persons with borderline personality organization are especially likely to use splitting, denial, primitive forms of projection, devaluation, idealization, and omnipotence to deal with anxiety stemming from object relations conflicts, but this does not mean that they will not repress aspects of a structural conflict. Although impulse–defense constellations often afford "no clear delineation of which agency within the tripartite structure (ego, superego, or id) was defending against which impulse within which other agency" (Kernberg 1980, p. 4), some of the conflicts of those with borderline personality organization can be conceptualized in structural terms. For example, we see in such persons repression of both an incestuous wish and any expression of guilt feeling it awakens. We can say that the patient is experiencing a structural conflict if, during analysis, he experiences his incestuous wish as coming from himself, and by identifying with it *owns* an object representation that acts either as a superego forerunner or as a primitive superego punishing him for his wish.

Kernberg seems to say that those with borderline personality organization do not experience guilt in a way that neurotics experience it, since the superego in the former is not yet a solid structure. I, however, have seen manifestations of very strong guilt feelings in patients with borderline personality organization under the influence of primitive superegos that are *owned* by them. What is typical to the borderline individual is the rapid disappearance of strong guilt feelings as he disowns the primitive superego and changes it into an unmended internalized or externalized bad object representation; when this occurs, he experiences struggle and tension between such an object representation and his self-representation, instead of having feelings of guilt.

Further evidence that patients with borderline personality organization utilize more splitting than repression comes from examining the total treatment process of such patients. One notices that, after mending takes place during treatment, the patient becomes "forgetful" of previously recalled childhood events; in other words, one observes newly established repressive functions. This may indeed be very dramatic. In treating neurotic patients, we see more and more derepression as the treatment approaches the termination phase. Borderline patients may also exhibit derepression, since along with splitting they also use repression. However, unlike neurotic patients, they exhibit "new" repressions in the treatment process.

New Developments for the Future

Many analysts have observed defensive splitting in borderline patients, and I make no attempt here to review their findings to offer further "proof" of Kernberg's formulation on this issue. Their observations are usually based on clinical findings. We need to develop vigorous and systematic psychological test procedures to prove the existence of splitting among borderline individuals, but I know of only a few attempts in this direction by psychoanalytically informed psychologists. For example, a Rorschach scoring system based on Kernberg's theoretical formulations has been developed to assess the specific defenses of splitting, idealization, devaluation, projective identification, and denial (Lerner et al. 1981, Lerner and Lerner 1982). These investigators conducted studies in which independent samples of borderline patients were compared with samples of neurotic and schizophrenic patients. They contended that "borderline patients present an identifiable constellation of defenses, different from that of neurotic and schizophrenic patients," and that "the scoring system is a valid means of identifying these defenses" (Lerner and Lerner 1982, p. 111). Schulz (1980) is developing a clinical scale for the assessment of the psychotic patient's ability to differentiate between self and object; this will further differentiate, from an object relations perspective, patients with borderline personality organization from those who are schizophrenic.

OEDIPAL AND PREOEDIPAL: AN ISSUE OF ETIOLOGY

Abend and colleagues (1983) would like to see greater emphasis placed on oedipal-phase conflicts in borderline patients. They state that Kernberg largely neglected this issue, but a reading of his work indicates that he does say a lot about the oedipal conflicts of the borderline patient. For example, he refers to premature oedipalization of preoedipal conflicts that lead to the development of a terrifying representation of the oedipal rival. There occurs a condensed father–mother image of an unreal kind. He also explains how, when oral-aggressive conflicts are displaced from mother to father, the boy experiences increased castration anxiety, and the girl increased penis envy and related distortions.

I believe that the issue on which Abend and colleagues (1983) differ from Kernberg is that of etiology. The former, while acknowledging the role of preoedipal factors in the development of a borderline personality organization, insist on the importance of the influence of triangular (oedipal) conflicts. Kernberg, on the other hand, clearly holds that the beginnings of that personality organization lie in the preoedipal area, especially during the first 18 months of life. The controversy, then, is the determination of what is dominant—fixation at the preoedipal level or regression to it. The oedipal–preoedipal dilemma has had considerable attention in psychoanalytic writings; Greenspan (1977), for example, asks how a *regressive* preoedipal conflict situation can be distinguished from a *pure* one.

Regressive or Pure Preoedipal State?

My work with patients with borderline personality organization points to some answers. If the regression to the preoedipal level occurs after the patient has established an oedipal or postoedipal state so as to have had enough experience with it, his regression to a preoedipal level is likely to stay infused with oedipal-level defenses and adaptations, and he will exhibit a strong tendency to make a consistent, however silent, attempt to move up again. At the outset of their treatment such patients may seem regressed, but the experienced therapist "hears" the presence of oedipal and postoedipal assets and real evidence of their efforts to return to that level. Only a structural frame of reference need be used with such patients.

When regression to the preoedipal level occurs early in the oedipal child's life, and if it is massive and involves many ego and superego functions, and if the child, for reasons such as being influenced by pathogenic fantasies or the lack of a supportive environment, cannot progress but can only chronically adapt to the regressive state, the difference between a regressive and a pure preoedipal state does not have practical significance. In such regressive situations, the child, when grown, will continue to use primitive defenses. The original oedipal trauma accountable for the massive regression can be disclosed and dealt with only in treatment. However, prior to this, the initial therapeutic work should focus on object relations conflicts, and the therapist may first need to consider a frame of reference pertaining to the internalized object relations theory (Volkan 1981a). I believe that regressive preoedipal and pure preoedipal conflicts can coexist. These patients enter the oedipal phase with unresolved preoedipal conflicts, which in turn color passage through the oedipal phase. They split the oedipal father's image as they did that of the preoedipal mother. Furthermore, in many areas the images of father and mother are condensed.

More importantly, I do not find it enough to deal only with the preoedipal conflict in treatment, and I do not consider the treatment completed until the oedipal transference configurations fully develop and are resolved. Further details of this process appear in Chapter 5. Like Boyer (1967, 1983) I emphasize *the upward-evolving transference* relationships that, in the long run, deal with pre-oedipal as well as oedipal issues.

REAL EXPERIENCES AND THEIR MENTAL REPRESENTATIONS

Meissner (1978) emphasizes that Kernberg's work concerns itself with *internalized* object relationships and not object relations in general. Kernberg's internalized object relationships "seem to come much closer to what had been described in other contexts as 'introjects' " (p. 588). Joining Meissner, Abend and colleagues (1983) point out that Kernberg does not give sufficient weight to the *real* experiences of the child with his parents, siblings, and so on, and that much of his work only emphasizes his hypothesis about intrapsychic development in very early life; the emphasis is on the developmental process and fixations within it. The developmental process will take its course, however, according to the nature of the subject's relationship with real objects, and it would be a mistake to consider that it takes place without such reference.

At times, in speaking about internalized object relations at professional meetings, I have noted a tendency for some practitioners to place unique emphasis on the developmental process of internalized object relations as though it does not take other processes and feeling states into account (i.e., historical events, unconscious fantasies). This is a rather mechanical way of seeing the internalization of object relations, and can lead to discussion of good and bad self- and object representations as though they had nothing to do with real human interaction. Were that true, all that would be necessary would be to help the patient to consider and confront both sides, and mend them! Thus it is important to remember that each good or bad image, each representation reactivated by the patient, has its own developmental history. To understand the patient, the specific nature of his preoedipal development and his oedipal passage must be examined; and the strength of his drive expressions, the formation of his self- and object representations, and identification with object representations at every level of psychosexual development should be considered. Internalized object relations, reactivated and dominating the patient's life as well as his posture in treatment, reflect a developmental response influenced by interaction with real people. That is not to say that when our patients exhibit aspects of these internalized object relations in transference, they are simply repeating what actually happened when they were children interacting with parents, relatives, and friends. Adult expression of internalized object relations is not a replica of childhood interpersonal relationships. Such early experiences must be taken into account, of course, but we must remember that they persist into adult life colored by wishes and defenses belonging to each developmental level, by infantile pathogenic fantasies, by changes of function in psychic expression, and so on. Moreover, real experiences modify certain drive expressions and prepare a mechanism for keeping the child's ego weak—or enriching his repertoire of ego functions and his ego's relationship with id and superego.

It remains true, however, that to understand a patient we must first examine the history of his early life. I will elaborate on this in the next chapter.

Chapter 2

Patients Prone to Psychosis

THE BORDERLINE SPECTRUM

Although Kernberg's description of borderline personality organization is clear, even a cursory review of the literature will indicate that there is no consensus as to what is "borderline." Stone (1980) offers a review of the ways in which the term has been applied, and, what is more important here, compares "borderline" as used in recent work with the concept of the state as articulated in the American Psychiatric Association's *Diagnostic and Statistical Manual* #3 (DSM-III). The "official" diagnosis refers to a broad definition including not only patients of the type Kernberg would call borderline, but also those in the Gunderson (1977) system.

Emphasis on borderline psychopathology seems to vary from one psychoanalytic writer to the next. Rather than offer a detailed review I will give selective references here. For example, Searles

(1977) emphasizes unconscious processes of dual or multiple identity, seeing them as a fundamental feature of borderline ego functioning. This view, I believe, is echoed in the remarks of Abend and colleagues (1983) that identification with greatly disturbed parents plays a prominent role in the development of a borderline condition. They do not speak directly of identifications that are contradictory, that cannot possibly be brought together, or that tax the individual's integrative functions (I emphasize the importance of contradictory identifications), nor are they particularly impressed with the existence of splitting in adult life—it must be remembered that their patients were healthier borderline individuals.

Giovacchini, known, like Searles, for his analytic work with the severely regressed, offers a different definition of borderline disorder from Kernberg's, pushing "the fixation point somewhat further back, but not by much" (1986, p. 44). He notes that Kernberg views the fixation point of the borderline individual as being at the stage of beginning separation-individuation, and stresses the patient's poorly formed self-representations: "I agree that these patients do, indeed, have problems in their identity configuration, but I would add that their egos are more amorphously organized than the psychic structure that characterizes beginning separation-individuation—Mahler's (1972) hatching phase" (p. 44). Thus, patients diagnosed as borderline by Giovacchini are more regressed, their adaptive functions more primitive, and their dealings with reality more inadequate. Such patients "make borderline adjustments to the external world, in that their adaptations are inadequate to cope with the complex demands of reality and . . . may lose their psychic equilibrium and become psychotic" (p. 45).

Kernberg (1975) divided those with narcissistic personality disorder into high-, middle-, and low-level categories, the first of which includes persons with effective adaptation on the surface, and the ability to gain success in their social lives and to influence external sources to provide them with a dominant role over others (Volkan 1980a, 1981b, 1982b, Volkan and Itzkowitz 1984). Those at the lower level are closer in function to persons with borderline personality organization. Although Kernberg refrains from categorizing borderline patients as high- or low-level borderlines, some of his work suggests that he sees possible diversity among borderline patients in spite of the fact that they all exhibit splitting and related primitive defenses, unintegrated concepts of the self and other, ego weaknesses as previously defined here, and so forth. It is when he speaks on the treatment of borderlines that he becomes aware of the possibility of regarding those on one side of the spectrum as being "healthier" or more "analyzable" than those on the other. In general, Kernberg (1975) does not regard borderline patients as analyzable, and the main goal of his expressive, psychoanalytically oriented treatment is to strengthen the patient's ego rather than emphasize the total and systematic resolution of his conflicts. He notes, however, that there are different levels of borderline patients: "In every patient presenting a borderline personality organization, at one point during the diagnostic examination the question of analyzability should be considered and psychoanalysis should be rejected only after all the contraindications have been carefully evaluated" (p. 107). Kernberg (1984) later became more optimistic about the analyzability of some borderline patients having a certain degree of superego integration and few antisocial trends and evolving to the point at which neurotic transference is possible. (As I have indicated, my observation has been that aspects of neurotic transference appear from the beginning of work with all borderline patients, but it is a technical mistake to focus on the neurotic transference in the initial phase of treatment.)

I believe that we can see within the general developmental and metapsychological guidelines of Kernberg's formulation, "psychosis-prone" personality organizations (Gunderson et al. 1975, Boyer 1986), some of which are less stable than others. Such patients know where they end and others begin; they all have psychic boundaries that, while not intact, remain distinct when close to those of others, although with drugs or some other regressing influence, representations of others sometimes flow into the self-system through boundary flaws. The regressing influence may be psychological since these patients are quick to develop transference reactions to others. A female friend, for example, may very quickly become almost altogether a mother representation, and when this occurs, the patient may lose his psychic boundary to a considerable extent when relating to her, although he maintains it in less critical relationships. Such persons can be expected not only to exhibit psychotic behavior, therefore breaking with reality, but to develop psychotic transferences if their treatment permits therapeutic regression.

NINE PATIENTS

During the last twelve years I have treated nine psychosis-prone borderline patients. Although I may from time to time, for the sake of simplicity, use the masculine pronoun in speaking of the genus *patient*, six of the nine persons in this particular study were women.

Four of the women were between 19 and 23 when they came into treatment; two were in their late twenties. One man was in his early twenties, one in his early thirties, and the other just past 40. I saw one of these patients five times a week, the others four. Pattie, whose entire case is reported in Part II, reduced her sessions from four to three a week during the latter part of her treatment. Except in the first part of what I call Step One, all used the couch. The average length of treatment was six years, save one of the older women patients, who terminated after two-and-a-half years in spite of my efforts to analyze her resistance.

I consider her case as a failure on my part, in spite of her having been very ill at the time she began treatment, and, by most standards, unanalyzable. In retrospect I feel that I was technically in error for failing to make adequate preparation in Steps One and Two before actively confronting her with her conflicts and before systematically interpreting her genetic material. Since she works near my office, is reliable at work, and associates with people with whom I have professional contact, I do know that after her treatment of two-and-a-half years she was able to organize herself on a higher level, and I intuit that she has established a stable satellite state. This state was originally described as referring to a special compromise solution for problems of separation–individuation (Volkan and Corney 1968) in which the adult continues orbiting around the mother's representation. In the case of this patient I believe that I was such a representation. She stayed close to me, but not too close, handling the pull toward engulfment and that toward (pseudo) independence by becoming a satellite, like a moth circling a flame. I suspect that this woman uses much energy maintaining her satellite state, which enables her to be to a considerable extent free from object relations conflicts so she can manage her life.

Another woman, seen four times weekly, remained in treatment for more than six years before we agreed on termination. She had definitely improved, especially in that she no longer experienced temporary periods of losing touch with reality. I do not, however, consider her treatment very successful; before long she required treatment for alcohol addiction. Since certain members of her family had had an indirect influence on my personal life and on the life of friends of mine, I must conclude in retrospect that unresolved countertransference issues complicated my work with her, especially in the termination phase. Her case illustrates the difficulty of treating anyone connected with someone uniquely important to the therapist. There remained some loose ends in our work when we separated, and ten years later she sought me out to deal with them, although by then she was living at some distance. We had two sessions to review the loose ends, and these were the most moving sessions of my long professional life. My patient in turn expressed great pleasure and relief derived from them. Although I have heard nothing of her for nearly three years, I like to think that she continues experiencing benefit from those two encounters and the work we accomplished in them. As far as I could tell, the outcome of treating my other seven patients was successful.

In general, the nine patients exhibited intolerance of frustration, and most were involved in chaotic and rather short-lived relationships. Any long-term relationships were sadomasochistic. The man in his early twenties and the one in his early thirties were married; the others were unmarried but involved in temporary, stormy relationships with members of the opposite sex. The wife of one of the married men seemed rather well organized on the surface, but while treating her husband I learned of her masochism, which made the continuation of her marriage possible; they had no children. The wife of the other married man was as primitive as he. They had one child, but divorced, the divorce so distressing to the husband that he sought treatment with me. The couple had undergone supportive therapy previously; indeed, six of my nine patients had had various kinds of treatment, some protracted (see the account of Pattie's earlier treatments in Part II, for example).

Splitting was evident in the way these patients related to other people; their self-representations were split as well, and they suffered from identity diffusion. At the lowest level of the borderline spectrum, they evaluated reality in primitive ways, unable at times to distinguish between an inner wish and an outer reality. Their omnipotent expectations of themselves and others would rapidly give way to feelings of helplessness and rage. All had poor work records.

All nine of the patients under discussion, including the two whose treatment I considered unsuccessful, showed drastic improvement; from a metapsychological point of view the seven whose treatment I did consider successful resolved their object conflicts, moving up in treatment to oedipal-level issues, tolerating oedipal passage as well as oedipal competition, and developing high-level defenses that they began using adaptively. All seven attained stable goals in their relationships and in their vocations and learned to tolerate being alone.

Two of the women needed hospitalization during the first years of their treatment with me; one was confined twice, for periods of a few weeks, while the other had one hospital stay of two months. The confinement of both was necessitated by rage and self-destructive behavior, which we discussed during their sessions. I arranged for them to enter the hospital, and I saw them regularly in my office while they were inpatients; when on suicide alert they were brought there by a nurse, who picked them up 50 minutes after delivering them to my door. I did not get involved with such aspects of their hospital stay as medication or the time for their discharge. I prescribed no medication for the nine patients at any time, but the inpatients were given medication while on the ward.

PROGRESS NOTES

I have for many years taken extensive progress notes on patients I am treating, and I followed this practice with the nine, although I did this *during* sessions with only five, making notes on the other four after their hours were over. I now make notes during all sessions, eschewing the use of electronic recording because I find my own notes a more satisfactory and creative way of reflecting what takes place. I have become so accustomed to doing this that it does not interfere with my hearing the patient, with my own regressions, with my observation of my affective experiences with my patients, or with my ability to formulate the meaning of what is taking place.

I do not suggest that every analyst take notes during a session, as it may interfere with its benefits, but I am not the only one who follows this practice. Searles (1976) tells how the notes he took in the treatment of "a borderline paranoid woman" became a transitional object for each member of the dyad. In this situation, his own analysis of the meaning of the notes was necessary to prevent an impasse, but notes are clearly very useful therapeutic tools, over and above any psychological symbolism they may hold for analyst and patient. Greenacre (1975) speaks of the utility of certain kinds of notes, and Boyer (1986) states that his keeping "copious progress notes" make "review dependable when I remain confused following a session or series of sessions, which, I believe, reduces the number of analytic impasses. This viewpoint has enabled me to be more objective while simultaneously emphatic" (p. 27).

I read and study my progress notes whenever I feel confused or whenever I have not seen the patient for a time. When during session after session a patient refers to a particular dream, it is most helpful to have notes on its first—and subsequent—appearances in his disclosures.

Progress notes are also useful in research and teaching (Dewald 1972, Volkan 1984). My notes on the nine patients here, for example, make it possible for me not only to provide accurate material about the early environment of each but also to provide data reconstructed in the analytic process.

THREE TYPES OF EARLY ENVIRONMENT

I classified my nine patients into three categories according to the first few years of life of each patient, placing emphasis on factors found within the child's interaction with the early environment that influenced integrative functions of the ego. I accept the idea of psychobiological givens in each case, believing, for example, that some children are born with less tolerance for anxiety than others, while some are more prone than others to exhibit derivatives of the aggressive drives. Allowing for this, we should examine the child's experience in the formative years in order to understand better why certain persons are prone to continue splitting after becoming adults.

My experience with patients other than the nine under discussion here suggests that the three types of early environment I indicate also concern patients with higher-level borderline personality organization and narcissistic personalities. Therefore, we need to look to factors (i.e., constitutional) other than the nature of the family background in order to evaluate why some patients are more regressed and psychosis-prone than others. All such patients have had difficulty mending (integrating) their opposing self- and object representations.

The First Type of Patient: Single-Parent Relationships

The first type of patient has had early one-to-one interaction with his mothering person, but difficulties in this interaction kept him from completing the mending of opposing self-representations and internalized object representations at the normal age of 36 months. The mothering person may, for some reason, perhaps her own immaturity, have been incompetent in certain mothering functions; consequently, her child was exposed to repeated frustration and intense aggression. This kind of background corresponds to Kernberg's account of the genetic-dynamic analysis of borderline patients. The original pathology is oral; oral-sadistic impulses combined with anal-sadistic ones so greatly load the bad self- and object images that their integration with libidinally determined good images is hard to accomplish. Furthermore, the mothering person may have lacked aspects of ego function, so her child could not acquire them by identifying with her and accordingly had a deficiency in integrative activity and reality testing. The case of Pattie (Part II) exemplifies this: During her treatment she told of the frustration she had experienced as a little girl, and throughout her life she maintained oral images of herself that were greedy, voracious, and murderous, like the animated mouths of the video game "Pac-Man." In time she came to understand that her mother had certain ego weaknesses, as when she continued to see a certain tree as living long after it died.

On the other hand, the mother may have been able to provide a model for her child in respect to reality testing and integrative activities but because of illness or some other circumstance she was unavailable. Or she may have been burdened by another pregnancy in the first year of the patient's life, or by an ill child. In such cases the patient might accumulate oral envy and aggression and have in consequence bad self- and object images heavily laden with aggressive drive derivatives and experience difficulty trying to mend his aggressively and libidinally contaminated self- and object representations.

To summarize, the first type of patient develops a borderline personality organization because of early noxious elements in his one-to-one interaction with his mothering person, and possibly because of a deficiency in his innate ability (a constitutional factor) to tolerate anxiety and to integrate opposing elements of the self and object. Six of my nine psychosis-prone borderline patients were in this category. In my supervisory experience I have encountered many others of this type.

These six patients came to the oedipal age with unresolved object relations conflicts that contaminated the father's image. I found the subsequent development of borderline personality organization among these children to be greatly affected by the father's role in maintaining unmended structures; they certainly brought to the oedipal level a lot of untamed aggression. On the other hand, the fathers had failed to help their children absorb the excessive aggression, reduce the ferocity of castration anxiety (in boys) and penis envy (in girls), and deal with the child's fantasy of murdering the parent of the same sex and being killed by him (her) in retribution. The sibling rivalries of these patients were also contaminated with intense aggression, and they never formed realistic representations of brothers and sisters.

In only one of the six cases completing treatment was regression from oedipal to preoedipal issues clear; preoedipal difficulties dominated in the rest, and this accounted for developmental failure and fixations. However, I found in treating them some elements that suggested original progress to the oedipal level with subsequent regression to the preoedipal level, in moves the patient involved customarily adjusted to. Such regressions were condensed with the original preoedipal fixations. The one individual whose regression from the oedipal level was clear in certain areas had oral frustrations and had displaced her dependency needs from her mother to her father, who not only met these needs, taming her aggressive drive derivatives, but helped her to evolve oedipal and even postoedipal configurations. However, his marriage deteriorated while his daughter was in latency, and he began stimulating her psychologically to a dangerous degree, taking her to the country as a wifelike companion, swimming with her in the nude, and so on. He left the family, as it happened, at the time she had her first menstrual period, when she was in adolescent turmoil, and when she was in charge of a depressed mother. She began to regress and to separate good and bad images of her father, winding up with so much splitting of images of her self- and mother representations that she exhibited marked borderline relatedness.

To some extent her treatment differed from that of the other eight patients; she went more quickly through the initial stages of treatment and developed a full-blown transference neurosis, which for a long time was dominated by reactivation of her original relationship with her father, her defenses against aspects of it, and her fantasies connected with it.

Typically, all six patients showed elements of oedipal-phase conflict, but it is significant that they were influenced by dominant preoedipal conflicts and that their reactivation was used to defend against anxiety if "hotter" preoedipal conflicts were relived. It was always necessary in treatment to deal with earlier conflicts before working on oedipal issues.

Many studies have added to our knowledge of how the family contributes to the development of a borderline personality organization in a child (Zinner and Shapiro 1972, Berkowitz et al. 1974, Shapiro et al. 1975, 1977). I believe that the patient groups in these studies represent the prototype of borderline patients, or Type 1. They note the failure of the family to provide a "holding environment" (Winnicott 1960) to facilitate the child's integration of positive and negative constellations, and they note that parents chose their borderline child to participate with them by means of projective identification (a feeling of being identified with the other, attributing to him his own qualities) in a relationship that embodies the aggressively contaminated self- and object representations they would deny.

These investigators speak also of regression in the establishment of the borderline personality organization, referring to the whole family group's regression to such preambivalence that each member seems single-minded in relation to the borderline child, even when he is adolescent and is forced, as it were, to absorb aspects of parental conflicts denied and projected onto him.

The Second Type of Patient: Multiple Mothering

This patient's background is characterized by multiple and contradictory manifestations of parenting that evoke multiple and contradictory identifications. The first type of patient, who typically has had a one-to-one relationship with one mother, may, of course, form multiple identifications with her representation because of inability to integrate pleasurable and unpleasurable experiences with her, but with the second type, experiences leading to multiple contradictory identifications are complicated by the *actual* existence of multiple parent figures. Cambor (1969) was, as far as I know, the first analyst to write on the influence of multiple mothering on a child's ability to integrate:

> There is . . . a greater tendency for a delay in the establishment of stable object representations, and this delay may be reenforced by interference with the process of fusion of good and bad maternal object representations. This interferes both

> with the process of separation–individuation and the progressive maturation of identification processes, and encourages the regressive wish for fusion with the idealized good mother only. [p. 91]

In a one-to-one relationship with one dominant mothering person, a child experiences loving and frustrating experiences and so learns that the mothering person is sometimes good and sometimes bad in terms of gratification. If not exposed to excessive frustration, the child then becomes able to integrate opposing representations of her and begins relating to her with ambivalence.

The child to whom more than one mothering figure is available may move from one who frustrates him to another and thus need not experience pressing frustration from any one individual. Thus it is hard for him to see any "mother" as a total individual; if his caretakers differ significantly from one another or are inconsistent, integration becomes even more of a problem. Kramer's case of Simon (1986), an adopted 6-year-old, is a good example of this formulation.

> I know that the outcome of multiple mothering was far worse in Simon than in most children who receive their major care from someone other than the mother. But I conjecture that a split in the self image because of partial identification with two competing care givers may occur in other instances where the pathology and hostility of the care givers are of great magnitude. [p. 170]

The child with multiple mothering experiences his contacts with one "mother" after another as a kind of loss-and-gain phenomenon accompanied by sad and elated affect. As an adult, the second type of borderline patient repeats in daily life and in treatment various changes of affect as he reactivates in the here-and-now his relationship with his early environment. Such patients are occasionally diagnosed inaccurately as being manic depressive; examination of their mood changes discloses a rationale of loss or gain. An experienced analyst or therapist can then understand how such loss or gain relates to reactivation of the internalization of experiences with the childhood environment. With proper psychological treatment these patients respond positively to the clarification and interpretation of their mood changes. Patients who related to an adoptive as well as to a biological mother provide examples, but there are variations on this theme. For example, if the child had had an opportunity to establish object constancy with a mother who died, he may keep the idealized representation of her with which he identified. Then, if he has a stepmother, he will form a representation of her that in many ways is contrary to that of the dead mother; then the child identifies with both but is unable to integrate the two. This situation often is a significant cause of lifelong activation of the splitting mechanism.

One sees somewhat the same phenomenon in the case of a white child reared in the South by a black "mammy," as he assimilates their warm relationship with his self-system. As he identifies with his white mothering person, who, consciously or unconsciously, may regard the black mother as inferior, he will find it difficult to meld his self-system with his internalized object world. Smith (1949) has suggested that the Oedipus complex of a southern white child mothered by both a white mother and a black mammy requires adjustment that is simple compared to that involved in the early dual relationship. I suspect that a similar influence has been the way in which the British aristocracy, among others, gave the care of their young children over to nannies and had only limited contact with them themselves.

Certainly not all children who have multiple mothering will develop borderline personality organization or a narcissistic personality, but I suggest that multiple mothering tends to foster such personality organization and has been seen to lay the background for pathology. Some children are more adaptive than others to dealing with multiple mothering and do not show adverse effects. One of my analysands, a painter, illustrates this. Seeing his work and listening to his free association about his paintings made it clear that his paintings were psychological links between his early identifications with two mothering figures. The creativity and ability to form psychological links that he had possessed even as a small boy enabled him to manage his object relations conflicts. He was able to progress rather positively through the oedipal phase and did not exhibit a borderline or narcissistic personality organization, although he had neurotic problems and an obsession to be a peacemaker.

In traditional extended families such as those in rural Turkey, the classic child–mother relationship is enlarged to include experience with other "mothers." The child may not, however, experience one mother as incompatible with another, but rather as a continuation of the same mother. Even if the child does perceive his mothering contacts as different, Turkish culture absorbs the ramifications of this, so as an adult the individual fits cultural expectations and does not have a pathological personality organization. It is beyond the scope of this book to examine cultural phenomena that parallel clinical pathological phenomena; the reader interested in this comparison may turn to writings by Özbek, Cevik, and myself (Özbek and Volkan 1976, Volkan 1979a, Volkan and Cevik in press).

The father's influence is as important with Type 2 individuals as with Type 1. For example, Kramer (1986) tells how Simon's father was too weak in reality, as well as in the representation Simon introjected, to "wrest Simon from the two mothers" (p. 170).

Two of the nine patients in my study were Type 2 individuals, and I saw others in my supervisory work. One such individual was a man named Clark.

> As a child, Clark had "many mothers" and multiple fathers, and the effect of this on his personality organization and behavior became clear during his analysis. He was a 27-year-old university student when he began analysis. He was married but had no children. He sought treatment because of a sense of dissatisfaction with his "inner balance," having "lost himself" from time to time when experiencing feelings of panic. He thought his main problem concerned his relations with others, which he tried in a primitive way to control. For example, he experienced his extramarital sexual adventures as being split off from his marital life, and at times he lost the boundaries between his self-representation and the representation of a woman. Although he would experience this as "a mystical, blissful union," he was very aggressive with his wife and occasionally beat her. These presenting symptoms suggested object relations conflicts, difficulty in

integrating opposing self- and object representations, and a susceptibility to having brief, psychotic experiences of fusion.

An illegitimate child, he had lived with his biological mother for his first 13 months. Although his father had rejected him and the mother, he was adopted by a childless, married brother of the father, after which time he had no further contact with his biological mother. His biological father became his "uncle" and lived nearby, although remaining emotionally distant from the child. While in his early teens, Clark learned of his parentage from his adoptive father, whom he continued to call "Father," and to whom I will refer likewise.

His adoptive mother died of cancer when Clark was three and a half, and he brought to treatment some memories of her as she had been in her terminal illness. She seems to have been musical and of a warm temperament, and when she died, Clark grew close to his father. But when Clark was 5, his father married a beautiful girl 15 years his junior, who took no interest in the boy. The second marriage had a bad effect on the father, who became withdrawn, easily provoked to anger, and a heavy drinker. When Clark became adolescent, his father's young wife became "repulsively seductive" toward him. The boy excelled in elementary school and was a favorite of his teacher. He was a lifelong student but felt disappointed in not achieving more. He married a social worker but continued his extramarital affairs.

By having relations with many women he was repeating his childhood experiences with multiple parents. Just as he kept his several parenting persons compartmentalized in his mind, he kept his women separate, on occasion fusing himself with the representation of one, and then with that of another. Once in his analysis he also split off the representation of his analyst. He sometimes experienced his analyst as a teacher who was idealized, but then as one who was devalued. Sometimes the analyst definitely became the precursor of a bad superego, or a rejecting object representation, and at such times Clark would refer to him as "an analyzing machine." He told the analyst how his image of him changed frequently. When it was bad, Clark would behave as though he did not hear him or accept what he had to say. This behavior, I believe, reflected Clark's defense against introjecting the bad analyst (his voice).

After Clark had been in treatment for two years, his wife bore a son, Sam. By focusing on the new father's reactions to his baby son, and the fantasies he had about him, we may grasp how his own early experiences influenced his personality organization, and how Clark reactivated those early experiences, which were contaminated with wishes, fantasies, and defenses. Although he had been rather calm during the pregnancy, he told the analyst that the expected baby would somehow be in danger. After Sam's birth, Clark formed through projective identification "immediate contact" with him; in his mind, the baby was, alternately and simultaneously, Clark himself. Both young parents became hypochondriacal about the infant, having him checked and rechecked by physicians.

The marriage foundered, and with Clark's reactivation of his early experiences, sexual activity came to a stop. He became a "good" mother and gave the baby motherly care, while his wife became the "bad" mother of the infant, who represented the needy infant Clark. He did not want her to look after their baby, and she became depressed and suicidal, eventually starting analysis herself. Against opposition, she continued to breast-feed Sam for 15 months. Clark, very angry, told his analyst of his desire to have breasts in order to be the perfect, idealized mother for his child. Unable to do this, he accused his wife (the antithesis of the idealized mother) of starving the baby.

During this phase of his analysis, he was helped to understand how multiple contradictory parental representations from his childhood, and corresponding representations of his own self as a child, were being reactivated. Clark came to believe that he had been breast-fed by his biological mother, and that, in an imaginative reversal, she had sucked his penis to give him pleasure. He began to speak more and more of the desire to experience fellatio while lying in warm water. This was connected with his adoptive father's oft-repeated account of his having wet the bed nightly after being adopted. His idea was that when he had been with his biological mother she had cared for him, changed his diapers, touched his penis, and made him feel warm and cozy. The analyst made the interpretation that his patient's wish to have fellatio while in warm water was a wish to keep a bond with his biological mother; before this interpretation was offered, a working through of the patient's childhood conflicts had obviously taken place, but it was the interpretation that moved him. He could now more clearly separate the representation of his biological mother from his internal gallery of multiple parents and could experience her in a more realistic and integrated way. In reviewing the knowledge he had of her, he no longer thought of her as either a whore or "eternally good," but as a young woman in a difficult life situation with an illegitimate son. He was now able to integrate more effectively, and in turn he could stop relating through projective identification to Sam, now a year old. When psychically separated from the baby, who was now better integrated in his mind, Clark could see humor (a good prognostic sign) in the previous pathological relationship between them. He called it his old "Samiosis," in a play on words related to symbiosis.

The Third Type of Patient: Deposited Representations

To me, he is the most fascinating. In this type, the ability to integrate opposing self- and object representations is taxed, because, as a child, the individual had experienced himself as a depository of a representation of someone else as it existed in the mind of his parents. I have compared the transmission of anxiety from mother to child with the transmission of germs that cause infection; and the passage of unassimilated self- and object representations and their affect dispositions from parent to child, with the inheritance of genes (Volkan 1981c).

I deal for the first time with the concept of "generational continuity" in my book *Cyprus—War and Adaptation* (Volkan 1979a); I saw this phenomenon in myself as I watched a military parade with my little son during the first anniversary of the 1974 landing of Turkish troops from the mainland on the island of Cyprus, my birthplace. I then recognized that I was a link between the representation of my father, who had died during the turmoil between the two ethnic groups in Cyprus, and my son, the grandson he never saw. As I watched the Turkish troops parade, and the Cypriot Turks respond to them with joy and excitement, I sensed within myself a representation of my Cypriot Turkish father, not as an identification but as an object representation relating to his grandson, whom I also felt within me. I experienced my father's representation as if it were alive. It was freed from oppression, as in reality my father would now be, due to the changed political situation on the island. Although transient, this was a peculiar experience, and one that other second-generation people experience. Returning to this theme later (Volkan 1981c), I wrote of my patient Linda, who exemplified generational continuity in a longer-lasting and more complicated way. Her father was involved in complicated mourning over the death of his 7-year-old only son. Linda, a daughter of a subsequent marriage, had a mission to make him forget his grief; she kept within herself the representation of the dead boy, whom she had never seen, and identified with it to a considerable extent. When she had a son, who was now of the third generation, she perceived him, at least for a while, as a representative of her father's dead son, and as a solace to the representation of her dead father she kept alive within herself.

In neither my case nor Linda's did issues pertaining to generational continuity lead to the full-blown pathology of borderline personality. The representation of my dead father relating to that of his grandson was activated in an intensely emotional atmosphere and was temporary. In Linda's case, the representation of the dead boy was to a great extent depersonalized and absorbed through identification into her self-system. Although Linda appeared very feminine, she was a tomboy, and analysis of her tomboyish personality trait revealed that it was connected with her identification with the dead boy. When she had a son of her own, however, the dead boy's representation was no longer so much a part of her identification system, and it could now reappear as an object representation deposited in her newborn child.

Such observations led me to search for those deposited representations of others that remain unintegrated and do not become a part of an integrated identification system, which continue to have a life of their own. Such phenomena contribute to maintaining splitting of the child's self-concept if he experiences contradictions between his developing sense of self and the deposited representation.

The replacement child syndrome has been noted in the literature of psychiatry and psychoanalysis (Cain and Cain 1964, Green and Solnit 1964, Poznanski 1972) as occurring when a mother who has lost a child bears one to replace it. I have tried in my work to examine this syndrome above and beyond the phenomenological concerns, focusing on a metapsychological explanation of interactions between the dead child's representation, transferred from the parent to the living child, and the rest of the latter's self-system. When the child finds no creative ways to deal with his dilemma, a foundation for maintaining the splitting mechanism is strengthened. Furthermore, Zuckerman and I (in press) have shown that it is not only the representation of a dead person that can be transmitted to a child by its parenting figures. We offer the example of a woman who had developed kyphosis at puberty, along with many defenses and traits to deal with the intrapsychic ramifications of her physical deformity. For example, she was phobic about any deformed persons she might encounter; through displacement they represented her deformed self, and she avoided them. When she had a son, she deposited in him the representation of the straight spine she had lost but had not grieved over, with all its symbolic meanings (e.g., a phallus) and related affect. Her phobia then disappeared, but she developed a new symptom—exaggerated anxiety about the possibility that her son would not be straight. During her psychotherapy with Dr. Zuckerman, her transference neurosis included her expectation that she would damage her therapist by making him a reservoir of her deformity.

One of my patients, Frances (Volkan 1981c), was a reservoir of the unassimilated and formed representation of her adoptive mother's dead brother. She was adopted as a newborn infant after her uncle's death. As a young woman this adopted child experienced herself as half dead and half alive; half in this world and half on another planet; half female and half male. She had, she thought, two layers of skin, and her body was sometimes invaded by "spirits" from another planet who were either all good or all evil. Although she'd exorcise them, she would await their return. She was obsessed with Poe's *The Masque of the Red Death* and felt at home watching movies like "Night of the Living Dead," in which eating (introjecting) the dead is graphically shown. I later saw a patient with similar psychodynamics, one of my nine patients. However, I would like to report here the case of still another patient of this sort, Maria, who was treated by Dr. Gregory Saathoff.

> A black-haired beauty in her late twenties, Maria was the daughter of a family from a South American country whose citizens considered themselves descendants of important historical figures. In a panic, she sought treatment after being abruptly rejected by a lover. She presented herself as an actress on stage and screen and an expert in pantomime; only after a few months did Dr. Saathoff realize that in reality she had never acted on any stage or screen. She had once gone to another city to take acting lessons, but after finding a drama teacher she developed stomach pains and went back to life in her parent's mansion. Even as a child she had acted as an entertainer for her parents, and as a teenager she assumed the identity of an actress from time to time. Dr. Saathoff saw her actress identity as a kind of armor protecting the real identity that underlay it. The writings of Deutsch (1942), Greenson (1958), and Searles (1986) on "as-if" personality are relevant here, as is Khan's paper on "the false self" (1974).
>
> On the surface, Maria's actress identity seemed an attempt to play the role of a noble and wealthy woman in order to maintain the family's illusion of still living in royal splendor. In reality, the family did have a mansion, but it was no longer full of fine things, being, rather, an illusory

skin concealing a certain shabbiness; Maria's assumption of an identity as an actress similarly covered up an inner deficiency. The lover who had rejected her had been involved with her in a kind of folie à deux, supporting her identity as an actress, and introducing her as such to people newly met. It was the loss of this support that had brought her to treatment. When she herself spoke of being an actress, she was animated and without any sign of depression, but underneath this armor she was fragile and very helpless, soft and feminine, and given to tears. She often spoke of feeling like a ghost, and having a sensation at times of sinking into the ground. Dr. Saathoff missed the deeper meaning of these remarks until, after six months in treatment, she revealed another "identity" than that of an actress, this time that of a daredevil. It surprised him to hear stories of dangerous escapades from the woman who had always seemed so fragile and delicate. He then learned that in reality she was a motorcycle racer, a truck driver, a white-water canoe guide, and a mountain climber.

Dr. Saathoff got the impression that her involvement in dangerous activities was accompanied by a sense of urgency and was a flirtation with death as well as a denial of it. "I can't imagine myself dying," she would say, and she behaved as though she were immortal; she seemed to be walking a tightrope between life and death. It was revealed, in fact, that she had had to deal physically with death: She had been employed in the transportation of corpses from isolated places by a jeep too small to carry a casket. As she sat in the driver's seat next to her helper, she had been practically in the arms of the dead body she was charged with taking into town. Dr. Saathoff sensed new meaning in her remarks about being a ghost and sinking into the ground. The story of her keeping the representation of a dead person within herself began to emerge.

Before her father married, his sister shot herself fatally in the stomach because their parents disapproved of the man she wanted to marry. The injured girl lived for a few days and would permit no one from her family except her brother to enter her hospital room; he was at her bedside until she died. We know nothing of the relationship between this brother and sister, or of what passed between them as she lay dying, but Maria had been told a family myth relating to the dead girl: Three days after her death a tree under which the girl would read was struck by lightning, and when her father went to assess the damage a scarf that had belonged to his dead sister blew out of a window in the house and wrapped itself around the tree. A week later a black cat appeared at the house for the first time, and the dead woman's mother comforted what she apparently thought of as a representation of her dead daughter. It then disappeared, but the myth of the wandering spirit of Maria's dead aunt had been established. In time, after Maria's father married and had his daugher, the representation of the dead woman was deposited in Maria, as clinical evidence demonstrated. Although the family kept the dead woman "alive," on another level they regarded her suicide as a blemish on their long and noble family tradition and kept her story secret. Maria's father had pictures of his dead sister in the home he established, and Maria recalled often taking it out to look at in times of isolation. Hearing her parents whisper about the dead woman, she had fantasied as a child that she herself was a reincarnation of her aunt, whom she was told she greatly resembled. Her parents saw Maria as a representation of her dead aunt, and this gave the child a conflict in object relations.

Since Maria's hair was lighter in color than her aunt's had been, they dyed it. They forbade her to eat mustard lest it eat the lining of her stomach; in a sense, they tried to prevent holes in her stomach since it had been a bullet hole in the stomach that had killed her aunt. Whenever Maria became anxious she had stomach pains.

As a child she had fantasies of having special powers and the illusion of being a great mimic, an entertainer. She wondered if she would ever die, and asked that if she did, her body be buried above ground rather than buried in it; this seemed to reassure her that she would never disappear. She told Dr. Saathoff, "I live under a curse passed from generation to generation."

When Maria reached adolescence, with its necessarily regressive position and second individuation (Blos 1968), the family myth that she was her aunt's reincarnation persisted. This interfered with her identification with her peer group, and, later, in late adolescence, with her formation of mature dyadic relationships. Overhauling her early self- and object relationships led to the crystallization of her identity both as her aunt and as an immature, fragile, and helpless "little daughter." Her real selves were composed of these two contradictory identities; the later identity as an actress, based on her fantasies of being an entertainer in childhood, was her false self, an artifact for linking the fragile child and the dead aunt identities, and concealing them. As an actress she could play both selves, without committing herself to either. Play acting lessened the tension of real confrontation between the two identities within herself.

As an adolescent she went to the place in South America where her aunt had lived, and was addressed in the street by a stranger who told her she was a perfect image of the dead woman. Her pretence—as an actress playing the role of her aunt—was threatened; she could *be* the dead woman! After this, she felt compelled to gaze for hours at her face in the mirror. The manifest content from her dreams at this time showed that she had two layers of "skin," like Frances, and they were in conflict. She tried to remove the skin she considered bothersome, or press the two together as if to make them one; this represented her wish to integrate contradictory identifications in order to resolve her object relations conflict. Whereas Frances, much more regressed than Maria, had hallucinations of being visited by spirits from another planet, Maria dreamt of spider-like entities from another planet who came to earth to paralyze their victims and devour them. In her dreams she would try to escape from them but would awaken and feel paralyzed.

In her late teens, Maria persuaded her parents to have a plastic surgeon operate on her nose, ostensibly to improve her appearance in order to become a movie actress; she was not conscious at the time of trying to expunge the "aunt identification" that bothered her, but while in treatment this motive dawned on her, and she said to Dr. Saathoff, "I still look at my aunt's pictures. She looks like the old me before my surgery."

Surgery for alteration of the body offers no solution for an internal conflict that is deep-seated and internally active. My work with borderline transsexuals who have had genital surgery shows this very clearly (Volkan 1974, 1980b, Volkan and Berent 1976, Kavanaugh and Volkan 1978). A male transsexual who becomes a "woman" after the removal of his penis and the alteration of his genital area may have initial elation from feeling successful in uniting intrapsychically with the idealized version of his mother, but he is likely to dream of the reappearance of his penis, and this ruins the good effects of his surgery.

Maria did not even have the luxury of initial elation, but had a feeling of horror when the bandage was removed from her nose and disclosed what she thought of as the face of a skeleton with two holes for nostrils. Instead of removing her resemblance to her aunt, thereby resolving her internal conflict, the physical intervention had made her look, she thought, *more* like the dead woman. She became deeply depressed and thought sometimes of shooting herself in the stomach, as her aunt had done. With the support of a series of male friends—who helped her keep one identity dominant, and the others suppressed—she was able to overcome her depression. When she became a daredevil, her co-worker, who was her lover, supported that lifestyle, and in that role she could be omnipotent and handle dead bodies and death in a counterphobic way, maintaining the illusion of her own immortality. When she separated from this man, she went home and spent her time with her father, who had retired, experiencing herself as a helpless little girl. Later her identity as an actress was supported for four years by the man whose rejection had made her turn for help to Dr. Saathoff. She told Dr. Saathoff that in her daydreams she performed the leading role only as a dark-haired tomboyish woman (the aunt) in a comedy (reversed affect). Then she would be world famous; everyone would recognize her and her talent as an actress. In other words, she would have the whole world to witness her reincarnating her aunt on the screen. Then she would abandon her career and retire to a farm that she described in idyllic terms as though it were a bountiful mother and live happily ever after.

I cite this case as an example of a third-type patient, and further mention only that in the second year of her treatment she became fully aware of her contradictory identifications, and, as though to rebury her aunt symbolically, she went to South America to see her aunt's grave. She was shocked to see her own birthdate, differing only in the year, on the tombstone, and realized that she had been born on an anniversay of her aunt's death. She had not been told of this and wondered if this were the reason her parents perceived her as her dead aunt's reincarnation. It seems probable that the birthdate was not the sole determinant, but that it likely had had an impact on the psyche of her parents and had made them deposit the dead woman's representation in her.

Chapter 3

The Therapist's Therapeutic Regressions and Countertransferences

THE ANALYST'S BACKGROUND

In working with borderline patients I discovered that my personality was compatible with theirs. I was born in Cyprus to Turkish parents, a replacement child named after an uncle idolized by my mother and grandmother, who gave me multiple mothering. My mother was the oldest child in her family, and one of her brothers had mysteriously disappeared while a university student in Istanbul, some six years before my birth. A body believed to have been his was found in the Sea of Marmara and was buried before being definitely identified; his brother, also a university student, identified the clothing found on the dead man and kept by the authorities. Nonetheless, a myth that my uncle might still be alive was fostered in the family, and my grandfather is supposed to have consulted a Cypriot Greek psychic to learn from his dead son what had happened to him. The psychic told my grandfather that six friends of my uncle had been involved in his disappearance. My grandmother kept some things that had belonged to him as "linking objects." Much later I described such objects as magical things a mourner keeps and uses as an external place in which the dead person's representation and related affects can meet the corresponding representation of the mourner and related affects (Volkan 1972, 1981c).

Although I had no conscious understanding that the idealized representation of my uncle had been deposited in me, I do recall comparing my pictures with his when I was a teenager. In one, in which he wore a high school soccer uniform, I thought he looked very much like me, as if I could see my representation in his photograph. I wanted to be on my high school's soccer team but was an utter failure in the sport. In retrospect I think my failure might have been in the service of an unconscious effort to rid myself of my dead uncle's idealized representation, but I think that in general I identified with it, though I had never seen him, and thus expected much from myself.

For some unknown reason I chose to write early on in order to sublimate the handling of object relations conflicts. When I began at the university in Turkey at the age at which my uncle had died, his representation in my identity system became bothersome, and I tried to externalize the consequent conflict by writing a play about a Cypriot Turkish student (myself) who went to the university in Turkey to look for six men who had murdered his uncle years earlier. When, after graduating in medicine and coming to the United States, I put together an album of pictures of my life before emigrating, I put on the first page a picture of my Uncle Vamık in the company of six unidentified university friends. Later it occurred to me for the first time, that in a sense, I "killed" him during my analysis in my own way, but I think I continued many aspects of his representation by making them mine. As a replacement child I was obliged to soothe the grief of my mother and grandmother, to be the "savior" of women with complicated mourning and elements of depression. I had grown up with rescue fantasies and have written elsewhere (Volkan 1985c) about their influence on my choice of a career.

Olinick (1969) wonders why an adult should devote energy to

years of arduous study in order to spend his days, hour after hour, with only a small handful of patients in what had been called an impossible profession (Freud 1937, Greenson 1966). Olinick wrote:

> I suggest that a powerful motivation for the psychiatrist dedicating himself to the psychoanalytic relationship is the genetic effect of a rescue fantasy having to do with a depressive mother, the latter having induced such rescue fantasy in her receptive child. . . .
>
> For such relatedness of mother and child to be formative, it must be early, though the necessary duration is not clear (see, for example, A. Freud 1954b, 1963, and Ferenczi 1923, 1933, especially 1933, p. 165). It seems that depression or sadness alone is not sufficient; in addition, the maternal character must be at least in certain aspects alloplastic. Often there is an effort by provoking guilt to force the other to rescue, such enslavement also confirming one's lovableness. [pp. 12–13]

Olinick adds that he does not mean anything as naive as that the analyst's "work ego" is nothing but a child playing at rescue; and I certainly do not say that my perceived compatibility with regressed or undeveloped patients should be reduced to the effects of being a replacement child. Olinick (1969) writes that what distinguishes the psychoanalytic psychiatrist is the degree in which he accepts regression "in the service of the other" (p. 14)—the patient—as contrasted with the absence of such regression. The analyst's St. George complex is sublimated, becoming part of his character without leading to regressive decompensation. But other factors also help analytic therapists to be able to tolerate therapeutic regressions of their own in order to "meet" regressed or undeveloped patients on their own territory. Such meetings are necessary in the type of treatment I describe here if the therapist is to help his patient travel on a progressive road and rise to a higher level of psychic organization. The more severely regressed and undeveloped the patient is, the more the psychoanalytically oriented therapist needs to regress more deeply in his psychoanalytically oriented treatment.

I feel also that I can understand my patients' rather primitive communications on the basis of my own experience. Although I was a city child accustomed to the amenities of the city, I occasionally visited my grandfather, who lived in an earthen house, and saw wheat threshed by a cow's dragging over it a wooden plank studded with stones. I remember striking such stones together in the hope of making fire. Since my teenage son can operate a computer, I sometimes feel that the symbols and practices recalled in my mind span the millennium from the Stone Age to the Space Age; accordingly, a trip into the depths of the primitive aspect of a patient's mind is not altogether unfamiliar.

THE ANALYST'S PERSONALITY MAKEUP

Here we need to ask whether the analyst or analytic therapist, if he is to be successful in treating severely regressed or undeveloped patients psychoanalytically, must have a special background of early perceptions and conflicts that although sublimated, are kept accessible and familiar. Little (1981) considers the analyst's personality makeup to be important, and Giovacchini (1975) notes *common* factors, certain characterological features, among analysts that influence countertransference. Searles (Langs and Searles 1980), widely known for his work with the severely regressed and undeveloped, is more open than other psychoanalysts in discussing the relationship of his background to his development as an analyst. Boyer (1986) also refers to his childhood, writing of how his father left him with a highly emotional mother and a single sibling. He recalls how his principal rival for his mother's daytime interest was a dream book—a dictionary of arbitrary meanings attached to manifest content—that fascinated her and that he learned to read in order to share it with her. He holds this accountable for his fascination with symbols, his intense interest in folklore, myths, and religiomedical practices, and an unusual ability to work with regressed patients.

Boyer, however, no longer believes that the ability to work with regressed patients requires exposure to and mastery of conflicts engendered by actual experiences with important parental figures, and writes: "I have come to know several psychoanalysts who have consummate skill in treating such patients and whose backgrounds were much more conducive to secure ego and superego development" (p. 13). Also, as supervisor of psychiatric residents and private therapists over three-and-a-half decades, he observed that "their personal analyses combined with teaching enabled them to develop a progressively greater capacity to work effectively" (p. xiii). I concur that a therapist need not have a special background with intense object relations conflicts, which he sublimates, in order to provide psychoanalytical treatment for schizophrenic, borderline, or narcissistic patients. After all, it is inevitable that all children have object relations conflicts as they climb the developmental ladder, and the ability to regress in the service of the other in order to grasp preoedipal ways of communicating is available to all. There are a number of factors to explain why some therapists can regress therapeutically more deeply than others, as is abundantly evident in supervising the psychoanalytic or psychoanalytically oriented therapy of either analyzed or unanalyzed practitioners.

Training analysis does not necessarily prepare for deep therapeutic regression, but it certainly helps. Assuming that the analyst functioned on a neurotic level, or with higher-level character pathology, before his training analysis, he can be expected to be familiar during his analysis with his own transference projections and his analyst's reactions to them; thus the candidate for training learns by identifying with his own analyst how to entertain these projections and still remain in the therapeutic position. Such tolerance is part of his professional identity. His own transference projections are on an oedipal level; when they include preoedipal concerns, these appear mostly as part of a defensive regression from oedipal conflict. Thus a neurotic or high-level psychoanalytic candidate may not have enough exposure to activation of primitive psychic constellations, chronic object relations conflicts, or the handling of such phenomena.

Regression in the Service of the Other

Olinick (1969) describes regression in the service of the other:

> Immersion in the needs of a regressed or undeveloped person necessarily entails a regression, whether as parent, teacher, or therapist. Such regression in the service and interests of the other's development is controlled, partial, and reversible. It is concerned not with the patient's immediate gratifications but with his ultimate ones; not with the myriad secondary effects of frustration but with the development of tolerance for frustration . . . the analyst "serves," through the use of empathy as a by-product of a controlled regression, to comprehend the patient and to impart this understanding to him. [p. 8]

Introjective-Projective Relatedness

This is accompanied in the therapeutic setting by an introjective-projective relatedness between the analyst and the patient (Volkan 1968, 1976, 1981a, Olinick 1980). I use the term *introjective-projective relatedness* in a general sense to refer to all inner and outer flow. It includes introjection, projective identification (Klein 1946, 1955), introject formation, and different forms of identification. Conversely, it also includes externalization of self- and object images (Novick and Kelly 1970), and various levels of projections. Rapaport (1952) describes different conceptualizations of projection, envisioning a continuum . . .

> extending from the externalization of a specific type of tension in paranoid projections, to that of any kind of tension in infantile projection, to that of a whole system of attitudes and tension in transference phenomena, to where it imperceptibly shades into the externalization in the form of a 'private world' defined by the organizing principles of one's personality. [p. 463]

(See Volkan 1982a for a review of the many concepts pertaining to the term *introjective-projective relatedness.*)

The Question of Suitability

Some therapists and analysts simply do not feel comfortable working with patients who are extremely regressed and/or undeveloped, and who inevitably require in treatment a corresponding but controlled regression from the analyst or therapist and an intense involvement in introjective-projective relatedness. I strongly believe that not every analyst or therapist should feel obligated to work intensively with severely regressed persons.

> Most of us feel comfortable in the treatment situation when we see a low-level behavior pattern such as a hallucination in a patient, unless this behavior is accompanied by an emotion such as hostility directed toward us. One reason we can feel comfortable is that our own "normal" behavior pattern is so far removed from the observably "crazy" pattern of the patient. We do not identify ourselves with the patient experiencing what is beyond the range of our usual way of life. But to be a target for the externalization of the patient's representational units that are connected with untamed affects is something altogether different. Some therapists cannot "regress in the service of the other"—to use Olinick's phrase (1969)—when deep regression is required. Accordingly, some psychoanalytic therapists may be unsuited for treating borderline or schizophrenic patients in analytic ways that require their own regression, accompanied by an observing and therapeutic ego, in order to develop fully a therapeutic relationship that parallels the child–mother interaction. [Volkan 1981a, p. 445]

This child–parent relationship that develops in therapy with psychotic or borderline patients was described earlier by Loewald (1960).

The analyst or analytic therapist planning to work intensively with the severely regressed or undeveloped should have training and supervision before attempting such work on his own, even if he has a suitable personality makeup and the special background already mentioned. I agree with Boyer (1983) that an unsatisfactory state of teaching exists and that

> . . . many training institutions still teach candidates that psychoanalysis should be offered solely to patients with transference neuroses and that other patients should receive sup-

> portive therapy or diluted versions of psychoanalytic psychotherapy which largely exclude interpretation of the transference. [p. 196]

To be sure, the transference manifestation of those with object relations conflicts differs from that of those with structural conflicts. The countertransference of the analyst is different when he deals with the severely regressed or undeveloped from that appearing when he is treating neurotics or patients with high-level character pathology. If someone severely regressed and/or undeveloped reaches higher levels of psychic organization in his treatment, the emphasis in his transference manifestations will change—and the countertransference of the therapist will change as well.

TRANSFERENCE MANIFESTATIONS

We must remember that different terms are used in the literature to emphasize different transference manifestations of patients psychically operating at different levels. For example, those whose self- and object representations are not differentiated from each other exhibit transference manifestations as well as full-blown transference relatedness, and such terms as *transference psychosis* (Rosenfeld 1954, Searles 1963); *symbiotic* (Mahler 1963); and *psychosis* and *transitional object relatedness* (Modell 1968) are applied. Distortions in the transference are gross, and the patient's reality-testing ability relative to what the therapist represents to him seldom functions. The therapist merges as an external object and the target of the patient's externalization with other object and self-images.

Patients with borderline personality organization as described by Kernberg (1967) exhibit *split transference* initially (Volkan 1981a), until their split self- and object representations are integrated. I have discussed the circumstances in which, because of splitting, the therapist can sense the presence in his office of four, rather than two, players; the patient's "good" self- and object representations are there as well as his "bad" ones (Volkan 1976).

Operation above the borderline level, with splitting no longer a problem, produces the classical *transference neurosis* during analytic treatment.

Narcissistic Transference

Recent psychoanalytic writings also mention *narcissistic transference*, but not in the sense in which Freud described the withdrawal of the psychotic individual and his unrelatedness to the analyst. Today this term refers to the transference manifestations of the patient with narcissistic personality disorder. The nature of this personality disorder has led to the formulations of what are basically two schools, one championed by Kernberg (1975), the other by Kohut (1971). Kernberg describes, from the viewpoint of internalized object relations, the "grandiose self"—to borrow a term from Kohut. This grandiose self is a condensation of the real self, which reflects the specialness of the child and is reinforced by early experiences, and the images of the ideal self and ideal object. The grandiose self develops when integration of the self takes a pathological turn.

In this sense, a narcissistic organization falls between borderline and neurotic (or character pathology on a high level). In the narcissistic organization, primitive splitting also affects the transference. The grandiose self is split off from devalued self- and object images as well as from devalued external objects. In the narcissistic transference, the patient behaves as though he were the world's greatest inhabitant and as though it were the analyst's task to adore him. When he realizes that the analyst is not adoring him, he scorns him altogether. Kohut has beautifully described different manifestations of narcissistic transferences, except the reactivation of the rather hidden devalued self (see Volkan 1982b, Akhtar and Thomson 1982).

COUNTERTRANSFERENCE MANIFESTATIONS

Countertransference responses to psychotic patients may at first include the therapist's hesitation to be involved in the cycle of fusion or refusion (Volkan and Akhtar 1979). In 1961 Boyer made the then unpopular suggestion that a major cause of failure in the therapy of severely regressed or undeveloped patients was the dilemma of unresolved countertransference. He later (Boyer 1971, 1977) joined others (Hann-Kende 1933, Fromm-Reichmann 1950, Racker 1968, Giovacchini 1979, Grinberg 1979, Searles 1979) in stating that the analyst's emotional responses can be used with great benefit in the service of the treatment.

Externalization

A paper by Novick and Kelly (1970) describes the countertransference phenomena of psychosis-prone borderline patients before they move on either to more regressive or progressive levels. Novick and Kelly use the term *externalization,* differentiating it from projection proper, which is used to defend against a specific drive derivative directed against an object. When treating neurotic patients we often see transference projections side by side with transference displacements. The patient directs a drive derivative onto his analyst, subjectively allocating it to him while experiencing himself as the object of that drive derivative.

Externalization is an earlier defense mechanism, one pertaining to aspects of the self as well as to internalized objects. Melanie Klein's term *projective identification* (1946, 1955) refers to something similar in the sense we speak of it here. When the child faces the very difficult task of integrating the various dissonant components of his developing self-representations as well as the internalized object world, some aspects are

> . . . valued through both the child's own pleasure and, more importantly, the parents' response to one or another aspect of himself. Those aspects which are not so valued may become dystonic. Their retention within the self representation will lead to a narcissistic pain such as humiliation. . . . One solution is to externalize that aspect of himself. [Novick and Kelly p. 83]

I believe, as does Berg (1977), that all patients of the purely preoedipal type, once they are in treatment, initially include their analyst in their constant effort to externalize and reinternalize, making their analyst one split-off image and then another, while adopting for themselves one self-image after another, and so on. Externalization and reinternalization of self- and object images dominate in all preoedipal types, but the variety of such externalization and reinternalization depends on the degree to which the patient has an integrated self-identity and total object representations. Novick and Kelly always see "some degree of fit" in projection; they believe that what is projected always has a basis of reality. That is, the patient hangs his projections on some real event—a canceled therapy session, for example—and the projection of hostile impulses will always have some core of truth. This is particularly clear in the analysis of a child. Novick and Kelly see, however, and I am in agreement (Volkan 1979a, 1981a), that there may be very little fit between externalized dystonic ("bad") representations and reality; indeed, there may be no observable fit at all.

Once a patient's analysis is under way and the transference neurosis is manifested, we can follow in the usual analytic setting the transference projections and displacements as they are anchored in some real event.

> A neurotic patient of mine had a dominant mother who had customarily denigrated her husband. The father was accordingly perceived as ineffectual, and in spite of his considerable professional accomplishments my patient considered himself to be ineffectual as well. His analysis revealed that this identification with the degraded image of his father had been a defensive maneuver to deal with castration anxiety. As his analysis advanced, memories that showed other aspects of his father as a stronger man surfaced. This new development went hand in hand with his transference displacement onto me of his attitudes and feelings toward this stronger father. As might have been expected, they were accompanied by references to castration anxiety. In other words, to see his father as stronger was to expect castration at his hands and through transference neurosis, at the hands of the "stronger" analyst. His references to this were initially tentative, and his view of me as a castrator did not induce in me any particularly strong emotional response since my experience as an analyst had made me familiar in the course of my professional development and practice with being considered at times a castrator by neurotic patients.
>
> One day this patient, while lying on the couch, calmly told me how

> amazed he was to recognize the pattern of the radiator grille in my office. He said that his father, who had been a mechanic, had made grilles and had made a beautiful one exactly like mine for his own office. The patient thus acknowledged his father's manual skills and made him appear to be a strong man. After a deep silence the patient suddenly broke into a loud outburst of hostility toward me in which he cursed and raved. He made it clear that during the silence he had felt fear toward me, thinking that I could hurt him and take advantage of him. His outburst was in the service of warding off my attack. Since he was usually obsessional and polite, his hostility took me by surprise, and I am sure I presented the appearance of someone under attack, having a quickened heartbeat and the sudden sweat of alarm. Regardless of this natural human response, my emotions did not lose their signaling functions; thus I was able to think through the patient's use of the radiator grille as a means of displacing behavior originally directed toward his father–castrator. His outburst was a protective maneuver against his projection of his own murderous impulses onto me. Moreover, it protected him from the possibility of homosexual surrender to his father. The reality of the grille in my office and its actual or fancied resemblance to the one in the office of his father gave an anchoring point for the interaction that took place between us. Within seconds I was in command of my counteremotions. I chose not to tell my patient about them since such knowledge on his part would burden him unnecessarily, but in due course the process was repeated and then was interpreted to him. This episode is but one example of many similar events that occur in our daily work.

I must emphasize that I do not equate this kind of counteremotion felt on one occasion with what we regard as a manifestation of a full-blown countertransference. I use it here simply as a microscopic example of a collection of such events, the macroscopic correlate of which is the full-blown countertransference reaction to the transference of a patient.

The Analyst's Tolerance of Externalization

The analyst who is the subject of externalizations may lack, especially initially, the advantage of having an observable anchoring point in reality which precipitates or accompanies such processes; he is more at the mercy of what is attributed to him by his patient. He will, however, come to understand more of what is going on as the therapeutic process advances, and as he gains secondary process understanding of the affect-laden sensations he experiences as the recipient of his patient's split-off self- and object representations. Even so, his countertransference responses are more likely to be generally unfamiliar to the analyst dealing with a patient who externalizes. Experience with such patients under supervision can, however, give the therapist familiarity with, tolerance of, and the ability to use such externalizations therapeutically. I would not advise anyone to undertake such therapies without first having had considerable supervised experience with them. I recall almost literally choking when working early in analytic psychotherapy with a psychosis-prone borderline patient whose behavior suddenly filled me with unbearable "bad" feelings; I felt it necessary for my survival that I flee into the fresh air and sunshine, and I could hardly wait for her to depart. It is not surprising that this patient's first remembered childhood dream was of her mother feeding her oatmeal and choking her with it. During the hour in which I felt choked I had become her helpless self-representation, and, identifying with the "bad" mother representation, my patient had choked me/her. Were such interaction to occur now, I expect that my emotional response would be tamer because I am now familiar with such externalizations. I would still feel it intensely if I were sufficiently regressed to accept her externalization, but I doubt that I would lose my objectivity. Moreover, I would find a suitable way to utilize my emotional reaction in the treatment process. After accepting her externalizations long enough for her to realize that I could tolerate them, so that in her identification with my analytic attitude such tolerance could be assimilated by her, I would tell her, if she had enough ego function to enable her to grasp my interpretation, that she wanted me to have a firsthand experience of the intrusive mother. As this microscopic example suggests, I use my countertransference responses more readily and openly in therapy with patients who activate unmended self- and object representations. Countertransference can in such cases more readily become a part of the therapeutic process than in the case of a patient with a structural conflict. However, I emphasize that I am not in the habit of burdening any patient by disclosing too much about my own reactions, or by reporting inappropriate material about myself.

Total Countertransference

Thus far I have described countertransference as the analyst's response to his patient's transference. In practice, of course, we deal with a "totalistic" form of countertransference (Kernberg 1965) that includes the analyst's total emotional reaction to the patient. There are other factors over and beyond a response to the patient's transference that influence how we feel about our patients. It should also be remembered that countertransference is unconscious; we know of its existence through self-analysis of its derivatives, by naming our feeling state, examining our fantasies as they appear in our sessions, observing our nonverbal gestures or bodily reactions, and so on.

Countertransference in the Treatment of Neurotic Patients versus in the Treatment of Borderline Patients

In comparing countertransference responses of a patient conflicted in object relations with the countertransference of a patient with structural conflicts, I do not mean to deny that problems of countertransference may sometimes be difficult in treating neurotic patients; prolonged issues of countertransference toward a patient at the neurotic level can bring an unwelcome stalemate; however, they differ from those typically experienced toward the patient who activates unmended split self- and object images and the affects associated with them.

Examination of the countertransference will yield important clues to the specific context of the patient's image units being externalized onto the analyst. Reference to the initial phase of Frances's treatment (see Chapter 2) illustrates this. Frances was in communication with both good and bad spirits "from another world," sometimes feeling them existent within herself and sometimes seeing them invested in me. Her self-concept was accordingly fragmented and aligned in two opposing ways: At times she thought of herself as an omnipotent savior, but at other times as dead. She was sometimes a woman, sometimes a man. Her psychopathology arose from her having been adopted as a newborn baby by a family that had lost a young male member and had been unable to complete their grieving for him. They had also lost to spontaneous abortion in the fifth month of pregnancy a child of the dead man's sister, so Frances was adopted and given the feminine version of his name, being viewed as his reincarnation. Thus she was perceived by those close to her in her infancy as half dead, half alive; half male, half female. These incompatible aspects of her concept of herself could not be integrated when she was a child, and my grasp of how it had been for her then was revealed by the externalizations she directed onto me. I felt numb and dead when the "dead" unit was in me, and enlivened and saved by her when her early mother's object representation was in me. My affective countertransference responses began making sense as I learned more about the details of her life.

There is yet another difference between the transference–countertransference phenomena in the treatment of a neurotic patient and that of a patient with conflicts in object relations. The notion that the neurotic transference is strongest at the time the patient enters treatment, and that a real relationship comes about at the end of the treatment, is erroneous. Anna Freud (1954), addressing this issue, states that the neurotic patient enters analysis with an attitude toward his analyst that is based on reality, but that this becomes secondary as the full-blown transference neurosis develops. When this is worked through, the figure of the analyst can emerge once again, but "to the extent to which the patient has a healthy part of his personality, his real relationship to the analyst is never wholly submerged" (p. 373). (This same comment can appropriately be made about countertransference.) This description cannot, however, be applied to those patients who activate primitive internalized object relations. In such cases, transference distortions may be extreme at the beginning of the treatment, and accordingly may induce "unfamiliar" and intense emotional responses in the analyst at the outset, bringing about a situation unlike that in work with the neurotic individual in which the transference–countertransference axis develops step by step.

Chapter 4

Two Styles of Treatment

THERAPEUTIC REGRESSION

In view of our examination of the ability of an analyst or analytically oriented therapist to have deep therapeutic regression in the service of his patient, it is not surprising that some who experience anxiety in meeting a patient at the patient's regressive position advocate methods of treatment that discourage him from regressing therapeutically and avoid his own regression as well. However, with undeveloped and/or already severely regressed patients, the issue of the patient's therapeutic regression should be considered separate from the therapist's own ability to regress.

Two Treatment Styles

Here we face certain theoretical and clinical dilemmas outside the therapist's personality makeup. For the purpose of a discussion of this dilemma I am dividing intensive treatment approaches in such cases into two opposing styles, although such division cannot be observed entirely in practice.

The first supports keeping the patient at a level at which he can function *without* further regression, while at the same time providing new ego experiences in the therapeutic setting calculated to help him integrate his opposing self-representations and corresponding object representations. Therapists endorsing this style hold that if these already regressed or undeveloped patients further regress, they will become psychotic and beyond the reach of "the talking cure."

The second view holds that such patients need to experience further—now controlled—regression, and hence that the therapist should not interfere with his regressing to a level lower than the chaotic one already exhibited. Accordingly, after regressing so low in a therapeutic setting, the patient will progress through healthier developmental avenues toward psychic growth, much as a child does when in a suitable environment. Those advocating this approach know that already regressed and/or undeveloped borderline patients may exhibit transference psychosis when regressing further, so they embark on the treatment expecting to continue working through the patient's psychotic transference in hopes of his becoming able to recognize a new and healthier psychic structure.

Both styles are justifiable. A proponent of the first will point to the role of primitive pregenital aggression in borderline patients and the possibility of its reaching unmanageable intensity with further regression, perhaps turning inward or calling for the destruction of others, the term *destruction* being used here in a general sense that includes the ruining of the therapist's efforts. In other words, the therapeutic regression may lead to a reaction that is not therapeutic (Olinick 1964). Knight's pioneering work (1953) suggests that in "borderline states," the weaker the patient's ego, the more necessary supportive treatment becomes. His view proposes mixing psychotic and neurotic features in borderline states with a surface picture that disguises deeper psychopathology. His idea is that in stressful and unstructured situations, psychotic traits would emerge; thus his emphasis is on supportive measures. Some analysts continue to advocate supportive treatment for borderline patients (Zetzel 1971, Wallerstein 1986), but Kernberg (1984) holds that this is contraindicated and suggests instead what he calls "expressive psychotherapy." In spite of this, for reasons I will clarify, I classify his style with the first type. He maintains therapeutic neutrality, which he rightly emphasizes while by no means excluding empathy: "Technical neutrality means maintaining an equal distance from the forces determining the patient's intrapsychic conflicts, not a lack of warmth and empathy" (p. 103). He is aware that aggressive acting out or other behavior that threatens the treatment (or life itself) sometimes interrupts the therapist's neutrality but advises his returning to it as soon as possible.

Kernberg's technique mainly depends on the utilization of clarifications and interpretations. He agrees with Frosch (1970) that patients with severe psychological illness *can* understand interpretations; but, he adds, such patients, including those considered borderline, either distort interpretations because of their psychodynamics or cannot put them to use. Thus, according to Kernberg, "Clarification takes precedence over interpretations. This technical demand creates quantitative differences between expressive psychotherapy and psychoanalysis" (p. 103).

Kernberg clarifies for the patient the way he is using splitting and other primitive mechanisms of defense and distorting his perceptions while in treatment. However, what Kernberg interprets is *not* the reason for his borderline patient's splitting his self- and object representations, and he does not focus on genetic connections, which await advanced stages of the treatment. Kernberg focuses first on the elaboration in the here-and-now of his patient's *negative* transference, and he is criticized for his selectivity by Abend and colleagues (1983), who hold that "such predetermined selectivity produces an artificial interruption of free associations and constitutes a preplanned approach" (p. 196). They believe that patients with borderline psychopathology have equal difficulty dealing with libidinal impulses.

My initial work with borderline patients uses a technique much like Kernberg's, but I prepare myself and my patient for further therapeutic regression, whereas he tries to effect fusion of split self- and object representations without the benefit of a transference psychosis. He takes his patient from a chaotic state and helps him integrate his self- and object representations by using clarifications, interpretations, and, it seems to me, confrontations. Abend and colleagues (1983) also see in Kernberg's work "a consistent and persistent confrontation of the contradictions within the patient's productions" (p. 194). The loop consisting of therapeutic regression is bypassed.

Kernberg speaks of the gradual increase of the frequency of advanced transferences in borderline patients, but does not explain in detail what he does with the transference neurosis once it evolves. His main goal is the integration of self- and object representations and the consequent integration of the total world of internalized object relations, along with the integration of affects with the patient's relationship, whether real or fantasied, with significant objects. One gets the impression that once he has achieved these goals he considers his therapeutic work finished. He says, "At this point, the borderline patient may be helped to come to terms with the past more realistically, in the context of profound transformations in his relation to the therapist and to significant others in his current life" (Kernberg 1984 p. 107).

It should be understood that this technique is for those borderline patients considered good candidates for expressive psychotherapy, and that Kernberg has written extensively on the management of sicker borderline patients in a hospital setting. I suspect he might not consider psychosis-prone borderline individuals like those described in Chapter 2 good candidates.

A Rationale for Therapeutic Regression

"Getting well" does not always require regression. Boyer (1983) illustrates this in a clinical experience with an adult patient in which stable externalization and projection were employed. Once unwanted aspects were controlled and kept in a reservoir, the patient experienced and sustained better psychic health.

> While working as a hospital psychiatrist during his service in the army, Boyer was assigned the care of a man admitted to the hospital in a strait-

> jacket. At the time, Boyer was extremely busy with other patients; since he could not give enough attention to the man, he released him from the strait jacket and asked him to write down the experiences he wished to communicate. A week later, when the patient arrived for his appointment at the psychiatrist's office, he presented Boyer with two thick notebooks filled with handwritten descriptions of his aggression-laden hallucinations and accounts of his delusional experiences. Although the patient had received no medication or intensive treatment, he appeared to have recovered. He showed surprise when Boyer asked what, in his opinion, had contributed to this sudden turn-around, and he explained that his recovery was due to his having given his crazy parts and ideas—written in the notebooks—to the psychiatrist. He watched Boyer carefully while explaining his recovery, amazed that he was not visibly affected by having become a target for the man's externalization and projection. It seems that he was using the psychiatrist as a repository. He wrote to Boyer 10 years after this episode, assuring him of his continued good health and asking after that of the psychiatrist.

Boyer nonetheless agrees that we see in daily work with deeply regressed individuals the beginning of a lasting structural change when regression to earlier levels occurs, initiating a restorative move. Early in his career of almost four decades, he came to believe (Boyer 1985) that therapeutic regression is necessary for the establishment of structural changes in the patient's personality, and I have been influenced by his work.

It seems that Boyer, Giovacchini, Searles, and other American analysts who have had long therapeutic interaction with psychotic patients and who have tolerated and responded therapeutically to their transference psychoses, favor the second style of treatment for borderline patients, advocating the need for therapeutic regression leading to structural change, even for those who are psychosis-prone. I belong in this group.

As Jacobson (1964) and Kernberg (1975) demonstrate, there "normally" occurs a developmental split between libidinally and aggressively invested representations of the self and object; ultimately, the "normal" child becomes able to tolerate ambivalence. In a sense, this kind of splitting persists in people with borderline personality organization, but its function is altered and it becomes the dominant mechanism of defense. By using *defensive splitting*, this type of patient keeps his contradictory ego states and their affective investments separate from each other. Anxiety arising from object relations conflict is controlled at the expense of splitting (and related defense mechanisms), leaving the ego weak.

Therapeutic regression in such patients would involve regression at least to the level at which they experience their self- and object representations as undifferentiated, just as they would experience a transference psychosis. This would in turn be followed by progressive development in which self- and object representations would be differentiated, and the patient would experience *developmental splitting* in the transference instead of the previous defensive splitting. This would therefore give him a chance to mend his splitting as a normal child would do.

In my work with the nine patients, I sought to test my theory. My experience with them showed that a focal, controlled therapeutic regression in such patients during treatment is indeed possible, and that once it is accomplished they progress toward health. Our technique, then, should focus on ways of controlling this regression and minimizing the danger of global disintegration.

As Loewald (1982) states, "It is not regression per se which is therapeutic, but the resumption of progressive development made possible by regression to an earlier stage or to a 'fixation point' " (p. 114). Loewald goes on to say that we notice and analyze defense that interferes with this resumption. But he emphasizes that the analyst also *validates* the patient's regressive experience as a genuine one having its own weight, claim, and title "despite its incompatibility with the accepted normal organization of external reality, object relations, etc." (p. 118). To accomplish this validation, the analyst must have a corresponding "therapeutic" regression of his own, so that his patient is "not left alone" with his (p. 118). Loewald (1960) spoke earlier about the child–parent relationship that develops in the therapeutic process of borderline and psychotic patients on levels relatively like those of the early child–parent relationship. It is the regressive immersion of the analyst in the service of the other (Olinick 1969) that creates a dyad analogous in intensity and extended influence to that of the early mother–child unit and establishes a setting for a turn toward the resumption of ego development and maturation.

FIXATION POINT

At any given time, all levels of regression may occur in the patient, but we can refer to a fixation point in regression that is followed by progressive development, although the existence of such a fixation point has been widely debated (Lindon 1967). I am not speaking of those fixation points that might occur in response to the need to adapt to some specific trauma; my notion of a fixation point is more general, involving a global response through the use of defensive (mal)adaptation to the accumulation of problems in the development process. Thus such points refer to the developmental level on which there remain some unfinished developmental tasks. Atkins holds a similar view (Lindon 1967), that although we sometimes look for some traumatic event to which a patient has regressed, such a search may be unrealistic:

> It is not necessarily a question of regressing to a trauma or a traumatic situation but could be a response to an earlier ego state of psychosexual orientation and it may not necessarily be to a traumatic experience. Also it can be a regression to a psychosexual, psychosocial crisis which has not been resolved. [p. 314]

As I have noted, it is possible for a patient's condition to improve if he can successfully externalize unacceptable conflicts, as seems to have been the case with Boyer's patient; or if he is repeatedly given new ego experiences, as is done in some supportive therapies to exert a psychological influence on the fixation. However, the analytic way to deal with the fixation point is to have the patient regress below it, or at least to its level, and then to unlock it, so the unfinished task is resumed and there is an opportunity for its successful completion, such as would occur in the development of a normal child. I agree with the clinical observation that each individual has a natural developmental push, and that a positive outcome can be expected if the psychological infection is removed and the developmental task put on the right track.

THERAPEUTIC REGRESSION AND PROGRESSIVE DEVELOPMENT IN THE TREATMENT OF SCHIZOPHRENIA

It is self-evident that fixation points in already regressed and/or undeveloped patients refer to complications in the early developmental process. The regression such patients display is not newly entered upon in the service of the resumption of development, but is a chronic regressive state referring to a defensive maladaptation to the fixation point, the resolution of the developmental task being blocked by unfinished business. Even in these patients, further therapeutic regression will be necessary. Searles (1966) suggests that this is true even for schizophrenics:

> Because the schizophrenic patient did not experience, in his infancy, the establishment of, and later emergence from, a healthy symbiotic relatedness with his mother such as each human being needs for the formation of a healthy core in his personality structure, in the evolution of the transference relationship to his therapist he must eventually succeed in establishing such a mode or relationship. . . . This means that he must eventually regress, in the transference, to such a level in order to get a fresh start towards a healthier personality differentiation and integration than he had achieved before entering therapy. [pp. 338–339]

Organismic Panic

Pao's ideas about "organismic panic" in schizophrenia (1979) may be useful to illustrate even better the therapeutic regression and the resumption of progressive development in already regressed or underdeveloped patients. (This refers to schizophrenics, whose usual regressed or undeveloped states are lower than the psychic organization of borderline patients.) We learn from Mahler (1968) that when a child's anxiety presupposes the existence of an ego adequate to handle it, organismic distress occurs. Prolonged periods of organismic distress over the mothering person's inability to function as an effective external ego make the child prone to experience organismic panic later in life. According to Pao, this experience shocks the future schizophrenic into paralysis of the ego's integrative functions; loss of the sense of self is painful in the acute phase of schizophrenia. The patient emerges from this experience of shock with a drastic change of personality that is a determinant of the diagnosis of schizophrenia.

I wrote about the treatment of schizophrenic patients with intensive psychotherapy, noting how crucial it is that, after years of work and the development of transference psychosis or symbiotic transference, the patient visit, as it were, the original organismic distress of his childhood and face the terrifying affects he had not previously been able to tolerate (Volkan 1985b). We can then say that he has regressed to his fixation point. Even though such regression may stimulate memory and/or reconstruction of a specific trauma (Volkan 1975), closer examination will disclose that the recalled or reconstructed trauma, like a screen memory, incorporates a more global experience of the patient's childhood. After reaching such a fixation point he experiences sad affect as a result of his loosening his ties to the earlier psychotic personality he had for so long maintained. Next, both patient and therapist experience pleasure with "mutual cuing" (Mahler 1968), and this leads to fresh, productive attempts of the patient to identify with the therapist, especially in those functions that were especially lacking in the person who mothered the patient as a child. This indicates that identification is a prerequisite for progressive development after therapeutic regression. The more regressed or, especially, undeveloped a patient is, the more noticeable is his identification with the therapist's representation a predominant curative factor.

> When some specific area in a child's interaction and experience with important mothering persons has been neglected, it is only in psychoanalytic treatment as an adult with a core deficiency that he can develop an ego formation that will enable him to deal effectively with this area. Thus, when we speak of identification with the therapist's representation as a curative factor, we refer to one or many different representations of the therapist dealing with one or multiple issues. [Volkan 1985b, p. 148]

I have written of a young woman unable to say "No" to anyone she thought of as deprived (Volkan 1982c). In her case, the deprived person represented the depressed early mother who, because of her state, could not function as an effective "frustrator" (Spitz 1957) for her child. It was in our mutual regression that, in transference–countertransference, I spontaneously frustrated our introjective-projective relatedness and became for her a frustrator with whose representation she could identify.

Since schizophrenic patients are involved at first in fusion as they begin treatment, as well as in separation and refusion of self- and object representations, they require a therapeutic symbiotic relationship with the therapist (Searles 1966) until their ability to differentiate between self and object is firm. While maintaining his observing ego as well as his "work ego" (Olinick et al. 1973, Olinick 1980), the therapist experiences a therapeutic regression of his own in order to allow a full-blown therapeutic symbiotic relationship—a transference psychosis—to develop. Once differentiation between self and object is well established, introjective-projective relatedness may permit the retention of certain representations of the therapist as a "new object" (Loewald 1960). It is at this time that the patient repeats and tolerates the childhood organismic distress that originally blocked much of his own ego development. This is then followed by further identifications with the differentiated therapist's representation in order to enrich the patient's ego functions.

IDENTIFICATION WITH THE ANALYST'S FUNCTIONS

Whether or not the patient makes progress after his therapeutic regression will depend on his ability to establish new identifications with the integrative functions of his therapist. Defenses that interfere with the resumption of progressive development and validation of his regressive experience should be analyzed. Our clinical observations indicate that introjective-projective relatedness in the psychotic assumes the dominance of defenses against anxiety; and among borderline patients, it parallels the use of defensive splitting, being a stale way of dealing with object relations conflicts. (However, once in psychoanalytic psychotherapy, the borderline patient, too, exhibits exaggerated introjective-projective relatedness.) The inevitable inclusion of the therapist's representation in this stale introjective-projective relatedness does not automatically promote ego-building activity, but the therapeutic regression in such patients opens the way to new vigor and a change of function in their introjective-projective relatedness. Certain introjections of the therapist's representation may then be retained as identifications. Cameron (1961) speaks of finding therapeutically hopeful aspects in patients operating on archaic levels, noting that operation on such levels involves the equivalent of early partial identifications in ways unattainable by a more maturely developed psychic system. He added that these patients, although they are adults, could even internalize and assimilate new introjects (identifications) like infants. Hopeful processes do not, however, occur massively without further (controlled) regression, but unless preceded by regressive disorganization, they seem only to cover up object relations conflicts that may reemerge and continue to exert a pathological influence.

The Patient's Ego Organization

It is my assumption that introjective-projective relatedness appears in all psychoanalytic therapies but with differing clinical pictures and significance according to the degree of ego organization that the patient has achieved (Volkan 1982a). For example, if the patient is neurotic and has a cohesive self-representation, his introjective-projective relatedness is rather silent; it may appear openly in regression, but only temporarily, and usually it is accompanied by an observing ego; the neurotic patient does not fully experience it, as would someone with low-level ego organization. In analyzing a neurotic patient, the main focus is the interpretation of unresolved mental structural conflicts as they are related to drive derivatives and defenses against them that appear in the transference neurosis. In the background of this central endeavor, a "constant series of micro-identifications" (Rangell 1979) with the analyzing function of the analyst will take place.

Rangell refers to them as being the same as Kohut's "transmuting internalization" (1971).

In fact, the introjection of the analyst in a gross and exaggerated way, involving a personified part representation, that is, one made up of the analyst's penis, nipple, face, or voice, is an unusual phenomenon in the treatment of neurotics (Rangell 1979), and the therapist should react to it as such and seek to learn the reason for its appearance. However, if the patient suffers from what Hendrick (1951) called "ego-defect" neurosis, that is, he has a psychotic, borderline, and/or lower-type narcissistic personality organization, one may expect to see in treatment the open and continued appearance of introjective-projective relatedness. The patient will refer openly to the therapist's representation, along with–and in competition with (Abse and Ewing 1960)–archaic representations. There will be a "therapeutic story" of imitation, introjection, projection, and externalization, accompanied by incorporative fantasies and leading to identifications that will alter the patient's psychic structure and change his self-representation.

Upward-Evolving Transference

I agree with Boyer (1971) that once a patient's ego organization matures and he forms a cohesive self and an integrated internalized object world, an *upward-evolving* transference relationship will appear. The development of more mature object relations with the therapist will occur in a transference neurosis, and introjective-projective relatedness will fall into the background of this relationship.

Of course, there is the danger that the "ego-defect" patient and his therapist will be arrested in the cycle of internalization and externalization and arrive at a therapeutic stalemate because both are using introjective-projective relatedness to defend against anxiety. The strength of this early mode of relatedness makes it difficult to move out of, and the therapist may be handicapped in trying to do so by lack of experience with patients of this type.

Projective identifications, which are sometimes accompanied by counterprojective identifications, induce exaggerated countertransference phenomena in the treatment of "ego-defect" patients. Unless these are understood and analyzed they make for failed therapy. Normally, however, the inclusion of the therapist's representation (when it has become an "analytic introject" [Giovacchini 1972]) initiates integrative function that enables the patient to mend fragmented and split self- and object representations and to attain a more cohesive identity.

The term *analytic introject* applies when the analyst's representation as taken in is not contaminated by externalization of existent object representations, fragmented self-representations, or archaic fantasies, but gives the patient a model of analytic attitude. One seeks its depersonification in order to involve its functions in an identification (see also Loewald's [1960] "new object").

In reference to the treatment of borderline states, Tähkä (1979) says, "The therapist's function, analogous to that of the primary object, is to provide the patient with useful identification models for a belated ego building" (p. 130). In this paper, and later (1984), he emphasized the phase-specific psychoanalytic encounter of patients on different levels of pathology with corresponding arrests and disturbances in the structuralization of their personalities. He suggests, and I agree, that "therapeutic techniques which are based on established psychoanalytic knowledge of personality development and which have proved phase-specifically growth-promoting should be included in the technique of psychoanalytic treatment understood in a broad sense" (Tähkä 1984, p. 133). The psychoanalytic treatment removes the obstacles so that the reactivation of the patient's *developmental push* is accomplished and promotes belated development within the limits of the patient's natural potential.

THE CASE OF JANE

The case of one of my patients, Jane, illustrates the raw introjective-projective relatedness of a chronically regressed patient and her attempts at identification with the analytic introject in an effort to consolidate her psyche on a higher level.

In her four-times-weekly treatment, Jane, who was in her twenties, began by referring to her inner world, which was populated with threatening animals or parts of them, along with parts of human bodies such as eyes, faces, detached penises, and nipples. Benign images moved in and out among the terrifying ones. Jane felt that she lived in a poltergeist world in which objects were moved about by some mysterious power beyond her control. Soon after starting treatment she would ask me when she was stressed to look first here and then there, to move toward or away from the light; then she would blink her eyes as though they were the shutters of a camera. In a crisis, she would, in effect, create an introject, "developing" in her mind a picture to soothe her when I was not there. (As an active object representation, an introject strives toward, but falls short of, assimilation into the self-representation to form an identification. However, it strongly influences the self-representation and its relationship with other object representations.)

Jane then would use my introject, which was contaminated by her "all good" archaic introjects, as a child uses a mother—as an external ego–superego forerunner. At this point in her treatment, to "take my picture" was to remove me from the outer world, and this made her anxious. Moreover, my soothing image could readily be contaminated by her "bad" image and quickly shift from the "benign" camp to its opposite. In terms of my physical appearance, she was taking me in, in personified fashion, as a somewhat abstract whole or partial being. I was not yet being taken in in terms of my functions.

This patient's core difficulty was her inability to fully individuate. At the time of her birth her mother had been grieving over a slightly older child who was deformed and not expected to live. When this tragic child died, it was in the arms of her mother in a car taking them to the hospital, and Jane was there. Their mother's depression persisted, and her inability to be a "good-enough mother" dovetailed with the small child's sense of primitive guilt (a form of survivor guilt) to lay the foundation of her psychopathology. Like Berman (1978), I have described patients whose lives were organized around guilt over the death of infant siblings never seen (Volkan, 1981c). Jane's sense of primitive guilt was clear. She acted like a crippled baby for days during one period of her analysis and evoked intense "bad feelings" in me through projective identification. Since her mother had not been close to her in her childhood, her father had tried to compensate, but he unfortunately sexualized his interaction with her and overstimulated her, leaving her no choice but to be fixated in primitive object relations, with their attendant conflicts and primitive defenses.

As treatment progressed, her unavailable, early mother appeared in her mind in images of cancerous breasts, which contrasted with the images of good ones. Jane wanted to save me (Searles 1975) when I represented her grieving mother; she tried to leave peaches and apples in my parked car, which she found locked; thus, feeling unable to save me, she went into psychotic panic. She felt that the earth would crush, like an empty eggshell, if she stepped on it—that she would fall into a void inside. Acknowledging her desire to save, I thanked her and reassured her that I was in control of my faculties and that her notion that we were both without hope except for her efforts was a childhood fantasy. When she became able to hear and use what I said I made genetic interpretations of the fact that she was repeating an effort to repair her grieving mother by giving her her own breasts (the peaches and apples) in order to benefit from her mothering.

Jane then went through a "therapeutic symbiosis" (Searles 1966) as was demonstrated by her belief that the couch was a swimming pool. She would lose the sensation of touch in parts of her body. Her body boundaries would disappear, and she would fuse with the analyst-mother (the couch). Such fusion with the analyst represented a therapeutic regression from clinging to fragmented good and bad images. When, with therapeutic help, she came out of her therapeutic symbiosis, she seemed ready to work toward a healthier individuation.

In the third year of her treatment she had a dream that indicated that important structural changes were beginning to take place within her.

> "I was in a palace in front of a king. I told him I wanted to get married, and that he could help me. There were monks in the

palace looking over old law books, one of which indicated that I could not get married. At this point I turned to the king and said, 'You are the king; why don't you decide whether or not I can get married?' Then a vent appeared in the floor and drew in the pages of the archaic law books by suction. They disappeared."

This dream came after her attempt to have her cat, Miss Kitty, put down. She had been using it as a *reactivated transitional object* (Volkan and Kavanaugh 1978), a bridge between mother-me and not-me (Greenacre 1970). I felt that her desire to kill the cat was in the service of intrapsychic separation from archaic mother representations. This dream had been preceded by one in which she killed her father, which she reported in the same session. In a sense, she was saying, "The king is dead. Long live the (new) king!" The new king represented the structural change toward superego characteristics taking place within her; the archaic law books pertaining to archaic representations were disappearing while the new king was being empowered to decide about such adult matters as marriage.

After telling her dream, she wept, indicating that she could now grieve over what she was leaving behind. Within a few days she moved out of her parents' house to an apartment of her own. Just before the new king dream, while still in her parent's home, she cooked her own breakfast for the first time. In the next treatment session, having moved into her apartment, she asked me for Turkish recipes. Since I am Turkish, she was in effect trying to internalize the "good therapist" via her incorporative wish. Instead of providing Turkish recipes I helped her understand her anxiety over the separation from her parental home and, with the achievement of her newly found inner structure, the prospect of new relatedness to the world.

Throughout the next month, I felt comfortably sleepy during most of the sessions. Finally I realized that she was speaking in an unusual, monotonous way. She was symbolically putting me to sleep with "lullabies." She was the "new" mother and I was the "new" baby. She spent hours in the kitchen of her new apartment baking pastries and thought of them as being made for me. During this time she described her schedule of four hours a week with me as being "like that of a mother nursing a baby on schedule." Who was feeding whom was interchangeable in her mind. Sometimes she "fed" me and put me to sleep, but at other times I would perform these mothering functions for her in her fantasy. Such introjective and projective interactions were different from those that had appeared at the beginning of her treatment; they were much less contaminated with the absolutely "good" or "bad" images of her earlier introjective-projective relatedness. She was experiencing new objects in the service of healing and growth.

Soon her interest in me as an element to be introjected (eaten) changed from the crude and cannibalistic form it had been earlier. She became interested in me in more sophisticated and "grown-up" ways and identified with me on a different and higher plane. She began reading about my homeland and its people, taking a leap from eating to the cultural field. This led to her talking to me about the Middle East and Vietnam, where the war, to which she had previously made no reference, was taking place. She then began paying attention to world news, and developed what she called "adult interests." Jane successfully completed her analytic work with me in a little over six years. She is now married and as far as I have been able to learn is an excellent mother to her two children and a supportive wife.

PSYCHOANALYSIS WITH FEW PARAMETERS

My work with the psychosis-prone borderline patients on the couch gave me an opportunity to systematize the process of their belated development. My technique prepares for entering into therapeutic regression and I consider it necessary for development through structural change, new identifications, and subsequent integration on a higher level. At first I called my method "undiluted/psychoanalytic psychotherapy," but Boyer (1985) suggests the term *psychoanalysis with few parameters*; heated discussion of what should be called psychoanalysis can unnecessarily shift the focus from examination of the therapeutic process itself.

The following chapter focuses on the six steps of my treatment.

Chapter 5

Six Steps in Treatment

This chapter will examine the six steps in sequence, although it must be remembered that either internal or external events may cause the temporary reappearance of one already completed (or aspects of it). Sequential consideration makes for an overall picture of the total treatment process and illustrates the ways in which characteristics of each step often dovetail with those of another.

STEP ONE: THE ESTABLISHMENT OF A REALITY BASE

After the diagnostic interview(s) I explain to each patient that we will meet four or five times a week, that I will not prescribe drugs, and that he or she will before long be expected to lie on the couch. I further explain that the patient should feel free to communicate whatever comes to mind and whatever bodily sensations are experienced in any session.

The patient with borderline personality organization comes to treatment with many fantasies about the analyst, some of which are primitive, and many transference expectations. Even at the outset he contaminates the analyst's representation alternately with externalizations of good and bad self- and object images. After the first hours, in which patient and analyst are face to face, the former comes to recognize the latter as unchanging over time and tends to correct, to some extent, his initial distortion of the reality of the analyst and the analyst's therapeutic commitment and aims. A precursor of the representation of the analyst as "a new object" (Loewald 1960) or an "analytic introject" (Giovacchini 1972) appears in the patient's mind during the very first sessions. Many of my patients have told me late in treatment how important my initial attitude was to them. I hope that, as treatment starts, my attentive but relatively unchanging presence gives a reality base for the intensity of introjective-projective relatedness in the transference still to come.

Therapeutic Alliance

I try to focus on issues to help develop the core of a therapeutic alliance. For example, I tell the patient that his symptoms or behavior patterns must have meanings, and that we will try to understand them; however, I offer no overt advice or information about myself except to say that I am available during the sessions, promising no overt support. I see the undertaking of treatment as *the* most important step in a patient's life, and being so convinced of this myself, I usually have no difficulty in convincing him, even if he denies my commitment on the surface.

Initial Nondrastic Limit Setting

Whenever a patient looks at my books, or asks to borrow some, I say that we are embarking on a long journey together and I find it natural that he should be curious about me, but that if he were to try communicating with me by handling my books I would find it hard to be sure about his message. Although I know I will find his nonverbal communications significant, I indicate that in the analytic setting I will depend on what he tells me verbally. I do not chitchat with a patient, and I make it clear that my restraint in this regard is due to my desire to understand him rather than to be mysterious. If at the close of a session a patient asks to use my telephone, I explain that although there is nothing special about my telephone, I would rather he find another because I would not know the meaning of his using mine were he to do so. Then, during the next session, I search for his response to my setting of limits. For example, one patient whom I denied the use of my telephone opened his next session with a story about a rigid, ungenerous, and bad person. After letting him finish this story, I explained again why I did not allow him to use my telephone—my "rigidity" was in the service of our working together. Thus I differentiated myself—and, through this, an image of myself—from his image of the rigid, ungenerous character in his story. The verbal outline of what constitutes an analytic setting is important in working with borderline patients; neurotic persons take it for granted, but it is often necessary to push the borderline individual to adjust to it.

The Analytic Image

During Step One I emphasize my differentiation of my image as an analyst, hoping not to overdo it as an educational ploy but to give the patient an image of me as "a mattress to fall on" when he later becomes anxious in his complicated transference relationship with me. I follow certain routines from the very beginning, even if the patient presents a crisis such as losing his job. I may remark that his crisis may have something to do with our starting to work together, if this seems reasonable, but offer no crisis management.

The Noisy Phase

When the patient first takes the couch, I try to note his anxiety level, exploring the possibility that my being out of sight might give him the idea that I had disappeared—or even that he had "murdered" me. I observe such clues as his keeping a foot on the floor while reclining on the couch, excessive pulsation of the carotid artery, pallor, and the like. When indicated, I calm him down with noncommittal sounds in response to what he is saying, and in this way reassure him that I am still there. Boyer (1967) speaks of "the noisy phase" of regressed patients, including schizophrenics, who will not tolerate silence on the part of the analyst. I agree and find that my noncommittal sounds keep a patient from feeling deserted, or thinking me a victim of murder at his hands. Moreover, for the patient who perceives his analyst as all bad, such sounds "tame" the bad image, and the patient on the couch does not feel himself to be in the presence of an unseen monster. Likewise, if the analyst is perceived as good, his throaty utterance modifies his ideal image, and the patient does not feel that all he need do is to lie silent on the couch and bask in the sunshine of a quickly idealized analyst.

Clarification and Suggestion

I make reference to what I suspect is causing his anxiety, clarifying what is happening in the here and now rather than interpreting genetic material and transference displacements. When his defenses fail, the patient becomes anxious, and clarification, with suggestions about the therapeutic alliance, usually helps him continue treatment.

During the first step my main aim is to establish the core of the therapeutic relationship. For example, a patient might report at the start of his hour that he had seen a skunk and then mention that he had applied more than his usual amount of deodorant while dressing. At this point he is calm, but he refers again to the skunk, with which he seems preoccupied. He then places one foot on the floor, as though to rise and escape from the couch, and makes other anxious gestures. I ask him to consider the possibility that revealing things to me may be difficult, especially if what he has to convey could be considered by me as "stinking." I explain that we are working together and that I am willing to listen to anything he is able to share about what is passing through his mind.

The Patient's History

As indirectly as possible, and with few questions, I collect as much historical data about my patient as I can in the first step; I refrain from making interpretations about the disclosure of his history. Although I am well aware that there are likely to be discrepancies between what he tells me and his actual history, his narrative is important to my initial formulation of his dynamics and supportive to me in the development of an empathic attitude toward him. Obviously, as time goes on, the patient and I may change our understanding of his history. Step One concludes when I sense that my patient experiences me as one committed to treating him and relentlessly protective of the therapeutic setting and my method of conducting our sessions.

STEP TWO: THE FIRST SPLIT TRANSFERENCE

The second step is established usually within the first few months when the patient comes to his session because he wants to use the analyst as the target of his alternating good and bad self- and object representations. Not only libido, but aggression also binds him to his analyst (Pao 1965), who maintains therapeutic neutrality. This is not to imply that the analyst fails to convey empathy or other feelings for or about the patient, but that he refuses to gratify his infantile wishes. A breach of therapeutic neutrality will have a more devastating effect on an already regressed and/or undeveloped individual on the borderline spectrum than on a less regressed neurotic patient. It seems as though the neurotic person can "forgive" the analyst for a mistake, but those with borderline personality organization find it harder to be generous toward him.

It is usual to see a chaotic picture when the patient uses defensive splitting and other primitive mechanisms and relates to the analyst with introjective-projective relatedness. The patient makes the music, but the analyst is the conductor, correcting gross misperceptions, misinterpretations, and obvious distortions of his remarks and making it clear that the patient has resorted to these to fend off anxiety. This interchange involves what might be called "miniconfrontations." I allow major confrontations in respect to only two issues: the protection of the therapeutic setting and the schedule of sessions; and the prevention of the patient's acting out in a way destructive to himself or me. If a woman announces that she has a gun in the purse she is clinging to while on the couch, I tell her that one anxious person is enough in my office and that she must leave the room and return without the gun. I also terminate the session of a patient who arrives under the influence of drugs or alcohol.

Holding Environment

The importance of this constellation is that it provides a facilitating or holding environment (Winnicott 1960, Modell 1976) that supports the patient's regressive state without necessarily inducing further regression. Without making genetic interpretations, the analyst calls attention to his patient's psychic operations in the here and now. I call interpretations made at this point linking interpretations, borrowing a term from Giovacchini (1969). They link events in the external world to the patient's inner psychic productions. The process is like showing a patient how day residue appears in a dream. If a female patient fantasizes seeing blood on the ceiling of my office (my extension) as she lies on the couch and during the same hour speaks of having her menstrual period, I link the two communications for her. Similarly, I might link a patient's psychosomatic reaction to his having seen a threatening policeman on his way to my office. This approach shows the patient that there are psychological connections in the products of the mind and psychological influences on behavior patterns. It could be said I am making the patient more psychologically minded.

Chaotic Splitting

I call this chaotic second step the first split transference. Transference manifestations will inevitably include the splitting of representations of the analyst along affective lines, contaminated with the patient's archaic self- and object representations and interaction between these split representations of the analyst and corresponding split self-representations of the patient himself. It is not possible to interpret systematically the first split transference, because at this time it is rather chaotic; manifestations are not yet able to effect, in the service of structural change, the mending of what has been split. They are repetitious in the sense of failing to accomplish any new level of mature relatedness.

I bring this type of split relatedness to the attention of the patient in connection with some event outside the treatment itself that both the patient and I have noted and understood. For example, in our case it was very easy for a female patient to observe that when she spoke of her mother as a good person she referred to her boyfriend as a bad person and vice versa. When derivatives of a split transference are manifested they are explained to the patient not in the way of an aggressive confrontation or of an order to him to mend his opposing self- and object representations and affects connected with them, but in a way so as to increase his observing capacity. The analyst helps the patient to see how certain events, perceptions, and feelings are connected with or influenced by the inner and outer flow of aggressively or libidinally tinged self- and object representations. For example, when a patient externalizes an aggressive unit on the analyst, he may exhibit anxiety about coming to the next session and lying on the couch. This phenomenon is then clarified for him.

Unrepressed Oedipal Material

I have also observed that during the second step of treatment the patient with severe borderline personality organization offers rather unrepressed oedipal material and incestuous fantasies. This does not come, however, in any systematic way, and it cannot be systematically studied in the therapeutic setting. In fact, patients who function on a low level of ego organization and who have split or fragmented self- and object images use oedipal material as "upward resistance" (Volkan 1976). I usually pay little attention to such material at this point in treatment except to make note of it as a form of resistance—usually against conflicts of early, primitive internalized object relations. I agree with Rosenfeld

(1966), Boyer (1967, 1983), and Ornstein and Ornstein (1975) that premature oedipal interpretations—indeed, any direct attention to such issues—preclude the development of the preoedipal transferential state that must be worked through before the patient can reach a steady and classical transference neurosis. It is clear that this approach is different from that offered by Abend and colleagues (1983). As Winnicott (1956) notes, the natural evolution of the transference will occur without the analyst's interfering except to protect the therapeutic alliance and its setting, and without the analyst's attempting to teach the patient or to support him in his real life problems. Within a year or so, the third step of the treatment begins.

Dreams

I pay attention to dream reports throughout the second step, as I do in others. Perhaps because of my interest in their dreams, all of the previously mentioned nine patients reported them abundantly. In this step I locate the day residue and note ego defenses reflected in the manifest content. The patient invariably begins to see that different characters in the dream represent important persons from his childhood as well as different representations of himself, and that his interaction with them profoundly affected him. I refrain from agreeing with his designation of some of his important childhood objects as bad and some as good, but I help him see that he relates to the images of important others in his mind as he relates to important others now.

Identification with the Analyst's Analyzing Functions

Throughout this process the analyst notes his patient's attempts to identify with him. Since such identification in this step includes what the patient has already put into the analyst, it may lead to a vicious cycle. Thus, through miniconfrontations the analyst will help his patient to modify an identification with him that he considers nontherapeutic. For example, if the patient views the analyst's curiosity as aggressive because he projects aggressive drive derivatives onto the analyst, he may then identify with aggressive attitudes. This will cause him to exhibit aggressive curiosity and try to needle the analyst, gossiping about him and following him around at any encounter in a public place. The analyst must make it clear to his patient that he is curious about him and his verbal and nonverbal productions during the sessions only because he seeks to understand them, and that this kind of curiosity is different from a destructively aggressive one.

The positive identifications with the analyst's curiosity and other analyzing functions that occur at the end of this step have a sobering effect on the patient, and the sessions become calm. During this time the patient will offer insight that is clearly genuine; it is accompanied by unexaggerated but deeply moving and appropriate affects about his interaction with his parents and important others as a child, and appreciation of the conflicts in his object relations. My experience has shown that at this point in treatment patients exhibit therapeutic regression.

STEP THREE: FOCALIZED PSYCHOTIC TRANSFERENCE LEADING TO REACTIVATED AND TRANSFERENCE-RELATED TRANSITIONAL PHENOMENA

After going through the long preparation of Steps One and Two, patients with low-level borderline personality organization exhibit further regression and offer psychotic *therapeutic stories* (Volkan 1984). One such story is offered by a patient who, becoming preoccupied, continues disclosures of an event involving transference session after session. It becomes an affectively lived drama, a here-and-now version of a real or fantasized event in the past, which it may now be possible to deal with in a different way. Such stories involve considerable action inside and outside the sessions, action that turns passivity into activity. One can expect the therapeutic story of a patient with psychosis-prone borderline personality organization to include manifestations of transference psychosis and delusional relatedness. With successful treatment up to this point, the psychotic transference is tolerable for both partners.

In Step Three the patient usually goes through a regressive therapeutic story within a few weeks or months. With effective interpretation of this regression, in hopes of resolving unfinished business from childhood, the patient moves into a progressive development to a new step, and eventually mends his opposing self- and object units, becoming able to experience a transference neurosis. What is interesting here is that such patients develop "new" transitional objects or phenomena (Winnicott 1953), which have the potential to become a new bridge to reality (Greenacre 1970). The patient might return in Step Four to regressive therapeutic stories, but if handled properly, each regressive movement has the potential to help the patient achieve better organization once he returns to progressive development.

Clark, whose case was reported earlier, began his third step after his analyst's interpretation that his wish to have fellatio while in warm water was a wish to keep a bond to his biological mother, and after he had abandoned his "Samiosis" (his pun on the word "symbiosis" that he used to describe his pathological relationship with his son, Sam) he was by then more than two years into analysis; thus, it is usual for the second step to end with the patient's first genuine emotional understanding of the genetic factors responsible for the fixation of splitting good and bad self- and object relations. The patient then seems sober, and his grasp clearly real, neither distorted nor denied. Sometimes an external event will promote the repetition and working through of some childhood memory, stimulating a therapeutic regression to the conclusion of Step Two. The therapist contributes to the interpretation of the drama. In Clark's case the useful external event that led to reactivation and observation of his object relations conflict was the arrival of a son and his interest in caring for him. One day after the end of his "Samiosis," Clark babbled like a contented infant on the couch. His analyst was aware of Clark's therapeutic regression, which continued from session to session, and unconsciously he himself had a corresponding therapeutic regression meeting his patient at his regressed level and experiencing a symbiotic relatedness to him. He felt drowsy and even fell asleep for a moment. He was alerted by the feeling that he did not know whether words that came into his mind had been uttered by his patient or had occurred to himself in a dream. Both were caught up in this symbiotic relatedness and were reluctant to have to end the session and face the reality of separateness.

The Creation of a "New" Transitional Object or Phenomenon

I describe my fusion with a patient in Part II, and her creation of a "new" transitional phenomenon to effect differentiation. Coppolillo (1967), Kahne (1967), Kafka (1969), Fintzy (1971), Volkan (1976), and Volkan and Kavanaugh (1978) note that in some persons the transitional object or phenomenon persists into adult life, sometimes covertly, sometimes openly reactivated. I have found that most borderline patients persistently use active, covert, or reactivated transitional objects or phenomena. Perhaps this is why Modell (1963, 1968) suggests that borderline patients are arrested at the stage of transitional object *relatedness,* emphasizing that this relatedness has regressive and progressive sides that are directly correlated with the relative rejection or acceptance of the external object (see also Giovacchini's 1986 work on the transitional space in mental breakdown and creative integration).

I have shown how borderline patients also use their transitional objects to defend against object relations conflicts (Volkan 1976). However, the transitional object (or phenomenon) performs a progressive function in illuminating the bridge between mother-me and not-me (Greenacre 1970). The patient returns to it when ready to move out of the therapeutic symbiosis (the transference psychosis). In order to start moving again up the developmental ladder, he may create a new transitional object or use an old, persistent one with a new function. For example, one of my patients who always brought a bit of cloth to play with during her first year with me, resumed this habit in Step Three, but this time she would "lose" it on the couch and ask me to play with it. It belonged to both of us, and as we "played with it" (my play was only verbal), she began more and more to differentiate her representations of herself from her representations of me. Once the reactivated transitional object had fulfilled its function, she disposed of her bit of cloth with a humorous comment, bringing instead a new dress to her session, the material of which looked somewhat like the discarded cloth—the transitional object.

STEP FOUR: THE SECOND SPLIT TRANSFERENCE

Although the split transference that occurs during the second step is chaotic and impossible to study and interpret systematically, the split transference becomes in Step Four a part of the analytic working through, and it usually runs its course in a year or so. This split transference becomes the focus of the work and brings the possibility of mending the patient's opposing units.

When the borderline patient focuses on the second split transference, he pours out childhood memories, initiating affective discussions of the genetic determinants of what is going on in the here and now between himself and his analyst. Different images of the analyst, and corresponding split images of the patient himself, are visited or recalled.

Interpretation of the Genetic Material

In this step, the interpretation of the meaning of all-good or all-bad images includes genetic material as it appears in the transference and in the patient's daily activities. The three types of early environment noted in Chapter 2 come to the fore and the patient reviews his feelings, perceptions, and thoughts about the important characters in these backgrounds. The analyst's interpretations are retained with many effects on the psyche. Finally, the patient expresses frustration as he continues to use splitting in spite of his wish to "mend." The ways in which ferocious all-bad images bring annihilation anxiety at the time of mending is interpreted, and the analyst supports his patient's attempts to integrate opposing images.

Interpretation of Missing Hours

On a practical issue, I have found that borderline patients in this step are likely to skip some therapy hours if they split the representation of the analyst, seeking him out when he is good and "killing" him (by missing an appointment) when he is bad. When a like situation occurs during the first split transference in Step

Two, I set limits, telling the patient I cannot work with him unless he comes to his appointments regularly. In the fourth step, however, I handle the question of missing hours by interpreting the anxiety pertaining to the integration of opposing affective images of the analyst.

Identification with the Analyst's Integrative Functions

In addition to interpretation in helping the patient to mend his split representations with their affective contamination is the patient's identification with the representation of the analyst as a new object. Although identifications with the representation of the analyst begin to occur much earlier, emphasis is now on identification of the analyst's *integrative* functions. When made the patient's own, these functions help glue the different, opposing representations of the patient together, like cement filling in the cracks and fissures of broken rock (Volkan 1982a). It is the analyst's task to monitor what the patient does with the analyst's "new" representation, which is now involved in an *exaggerated* introjective-projective relatedness. Although this representation is still contaminated with archaic good and bad objects, the patient is now ready to see it in terms of gray rather than in mutually exclusive terms of black and white. On the clinical level, the analyst will observe the patient's renewed and exaggerated interest in the extensions of the analyst such as the office furniture, pictures, and the like. For example, the patient may begin to refer in an accepting way to some picture on the wall formerly perceived as monstrous.

STEP FIVE: THE DEVELOPMENT OF TRANSFERENCE NEUROSIS

Once the ego organization moves from a lower level to one more integrated, the patient moves from a split transference to a transference neurosis, as indicated. I agree with those who hold that the upward-evolving transference relationship of the borderline patient is made possible by the development of increasingly mature object relations with the analyst. Kernberg's statement (1975) that narcissistic transference gives way to transference neurosis is, I believe, true for the borderline patient as well. At one crucial point, the deep admiration and love for the ideal mother and the hatred for the dangerous mother meet in the transference. Depression ensues, and the patient may even entertain suicidal thoughts, Kernberg says, because he has mistreated the analyst as well as other significant persons in his life and may feel that he has actually destroyed those whom he could have loved and who might have loved him. If this crucial point is watched by the therapist and properly interpreted to the patient, the latter is likely to experience only deep sadness instead of depression.

Oedipus Complex

The vicissitudes of a genuine Oedipus complex are unmistakably present in this step. Although they may not emerge as completely as in a "classical" case, the patient now experiences the oedipal issue *for the first time with a mended inner structure*. Consequently, the experience of oedipal issues is fresh; they do not rise piecemeal from under a layer of repression. In a sense, these oedipal elements are like those the child analyst sees in children going through the Oedipus complex for the first time. Interestingly, with the development and resolution of these issues, the patient shows an increased capacity for repression, and some of the elements of split transference manifestations that are not mended are repressed.

STEP SIX: THE THIRD SPLIT TRANSFERENCE AND TERMINATION

The termination phase is extremely important in the analytic treatment of psychosis-prone borderline patients. If the "loose ends" are not tied, the patient might in the future, under certain circumstances, regress and stay regressed. By "tying the loose ends" I do not mean a rigid search for the perfect analysis, but only that there are last-minute secrets and/or activities that constitute a link to the regressive self and regressive operations. The termination phase allows such patients to bring these links to the surface and examine them, master the feelings they generate, and grieve over their surrender.

More than any other period of treatment, this sixth step approximates that of classical analysis in which the Oedipus complex has a "final" solution.

Little has been written about the termination phase of patients who had low-level character pathology at the start of their analytic treatment. Modell (1976), writing about the narcissistic patient, is exceptional. He divides the psychoanalytic process of patients with narcissistic character disorder into three phases. The last one, which ends with termination, approximates that of classical analysis in which the Oedipus complex is dealt with. Modell is quick to emphasize that the vicissitudes of the Oedipus complex may not emerge as completely as in a classical case and to say that, during this phase, the possibility of regressive movements is ever-present. To Modell's observations, I add (Volkan, 1979b) that the oedipal elements in the termination phase of narcissistic patients are often tinged with narcissistic glorification as the patient regards himself as "Number One" and thus behaves as though he is the only oedipal child in the entire world.

I deal in other writings (Volkan 1975, 1976) with the termination phase of the psychoanalytic treatment of patients with borderline character organization. I suggest that, even after the borderline patient develops a transference neurosis, the background situation (splitting), so turbulent at first and now resolved as well as repressed, must continue to have attention. I suggest also that primitive splitting returns in the termination phase derepressed as though for review, ushering in a third split transference manifestation.

Because of the importance of Step Six, I will explore it here in some detail. I refer first to the termination phase of a neurotic patient and/or one with high-level character pathology and then I focus on the psychosis-prone borderline patient, comparing his termination phase with that of the former.

The Termination Phase of the Neurotic Patient

The psychoanalytic literature suggests different criteria for starting the mutually agreed-upon termination phase of an adult patient who is neurotic or who has high-level character pathology. Glover (1955) asks a number of psychoanalysts for their criteria, asking if such criteria were (1) symptomatic, (2) psychosocial, or (3) social. Although all claimed to use all three indications, most admitted that they decided on termination on essentially "intuitive" grounds. Glover writes: "It would almost appear as if the use of systematic criteria were a source of guilt, as if only intuitive criteria were free of suspicion. This reintroduces the bugbear of unconscious and pre-conscious assessments of, and reactions to, the patient" (p. 327). Glover does not oppose an analyst's use of intuition but suggests that one should learn from experience the extent to which one could trust his preferred method, whether it arise from intuition or intellectual assessment, and devise suitable checks on his conclusions. Weigert's remarks (1952) on termination also take into account the analyst's self-observation, regarding the appearance of a freer and more spontaneous feeling toward the patient as an indication that the time is ready for termination. Criteria more readily examined systematically include the resolution of the patient's transference neurosis (Glover 1955, Hurn 1970); the resolution of a specific area of the transference neurosis; the resolution of the Oedipus complex (Miller 1965); the patient's coming to experience his analyst as a "new object" (Loewald 1960); and others. In Freud's writing we can find remarks about the criteria for "cure" in analysis, and for a healthy personality makeup, but he writes nothing about initiating the termination phase.

Novick (1982) criticizes those who hold that the termination phase proper begins when the transference neurosis—and, by implication, the Oedipus complex that was reviewed in the treatment—is resolved. He says, "If we wait until the transference neurosis is resolved, until all criteria of cure have been achieved, before starting the termination phase, then indeed there is nothing to do during the terminal phase" (p. 345). He suggests that the termination phase should begin at a point of maximum evolution of the Oedipus complex in the transference neurosis. According to this line of thought, much work remains to be done on the "final" resolution of the Oedipus complex during the termination phase. My experience supports Novick's views. In *What Do You Get*

When You Cross a Dandelion with a Rose? (Volkan 1984), which is a true and detailed story of a psychoanalysis, I clearly show how much work was done in the termination phase to arrive at the "final" resolution of my patient's Oedipus complex. Thus I suggest that the termination phase of treatment of a patient who is neurotic or who has high-level character pathology should last for perhaps three or four months, which is a reasonable amount of time for mourning by both parties of the dyad.

Before setting a termination date I usually spend three or four months helping my analysand to take stock and arrive at a mutually agreeable time to terminate. Dewald (1972) has written on assessing structural change at the completion of an analysis, and his criteria can also be applied to stocktaking. I agree with Rangell (1966), Ticho (1972), and Novick (1982) that the termination phase should be divided into two subphases, in the first of which a decision that the analysis can and should end is reached, and in which both the patient and the analyst take stock. The second subphase begins with the decision about the termination date. I focus here on this second subphase, classically known as the termination phase proper.

I usually work for three to four months with a patient after setting the date for termination, although there are exceptions. For example, I reached an agreement with a patient for terminating in three months, but I later considered the agreement invalid and ended his analysis in an unusual way.

> The patient's father, a ranking military officer, had left his family for overseas duty for two years at the time my patient was approaching the oedipal age, and while awaiting her husband's return, his mother had showered her child with affection. The oedipal boy then felt exaggeratedly competitive when his father came home. His mother would go into her son's bedroom, lock the door, and smoke while sitting on the child's bed as he tried to go to sleep. She would say, "My darling little boy, this [her smoking] is our secret; your father does not like me to smoke." For the child this was an oedipal triumph, and he symbolically kept it alive by keeping secrets, especially from father figures, for the rest of his life.
>
> Once we had agreed on a termination date, he told me a secret he had previously kept from me. After discussing with him what he was repeating—a secretive oedipal triumph over me—we cancelled the termination date. I told him that after we had worked through the meaning of his

> "last" secret I would tell him when we would be through with his analysis. In a sense I was asserting the oedipal father's strength so that in turn he could identify with a strong oedipal father. I hoped that by doing this we would prevent his going through life feeling obliged to have symbolic secrets. I ended his analysis in the middle of a session after a few more months of work beyond the original termination date. I have a 20-year indirect follow-up on this case and hear that he is still doing extremely well.

There are other controversies about how much time should pass in an analysis after the setting of a termination date. When symptoms return during this period, differing explanations are offered. Kubie (1968), for example, does not see the return of symptoms in this phase as an expectable, "normal" occurrence, holding that it is an indication of failure to resolve the transference. Miller (1965) believes it to be connected with the patient's attempt to retain the infantile fantasy of omnipotence. It is usual for my adult patients to exhibit some symptom revival, and I do not consider this an indication of failure; it is accompanied by an observing ego and does not lead to disorganization. Patients revive their symptoms in symbolic therapeutic stories. I see this as part of a last effort to take stock and, more importantly, part of the mourning process. Patients revive their symptoms in order to part with them.

Glover (1955) holds that the reactivation of symptoms at the end of the analysis is the patient's way of clinging to the analyst, and there is support for this concept in certain cases. Nonetheless, I find the formulation of clinging secondary to evidence of the mourning process.

The Termination Phase of Psychosis-Prone Borderline Patients

In the course of their improvement, psychosis-prone borderline patients develop a better ability to integrate and a better ability to repress. Their repertoire of high-level defense mechanisms improves. However, when they come to the termination phase, they face the biggest separation of their lives: the separation from their analyst and from the therapeutic process, which is closer to a parent–child relationship than the therapeutic relationship of a neurotic and/or a person with high-level character pathology. Borderline patients, like adolescents (Novick 1982), exhibit the recurrence of old symptoms during the termination phase more often than do neurotic patients. They reexamine their object relations conflicts and, more importantly, revive old ways of controlling separation anxiety.

There is a longer time period between the setting of a date and the completion of treatment in the case of a borderline patient than with a typical neurotic; I usually plan for a period of six months to a year. When manifestations of the split transference reappear openly—and perhaps exaggeratedly—in the termination phase, I do not hasten to interpret them or to bring up genetic material reflected in recent interaction either within or outside therapy but exercise instead an attitude of *benign neglect* toward them. The patient then will inevitably interpret the appearance of primitive splitting and related defenses, make genetic references about it and, what is more important, acknowledge his clinging to it as a way of clinging to the analyst. This is more the case in borderline patients than in those who possess high-level character organization and are neurotic. However, borderline patients also reactivate their symptoms after the termination date is set, as part of their mourning process. I help the patient to face his own utilization of his observing ego in understanding the symptom revival and make him use his own integrative function with little assistance from me.

These patients strongly exhibit separation anxiety when coming to treatment, and they tend to use primitive and "magical" defenses against separation anxiety again when, after much work, they face the reality of terminating and leaving their analyst, who must be aware of this possibility. Even when his analytic treatment has given the patient experience in grieving, in a hidden and magical way he may want to control his grief over terminating, perhaps using secret "linking objects or phenomena" (Volkan 1972, 1981c) to try to remain in a state in which the option of either "killing" or "uniting with" the analyst always remains open. He will then choose an inanimate or nonhuman object (linking object) or an abstract symbol (linking phenomenon) through which to "connect" his representation of himself with the corresponding representation of the lost object (person), thus maintaining the illusion of being able either to bring the lost person back or "kill" him, although he does neither and stays in astate of limbo. Although not resolved, the separation conflict is controlled, at least for the time being.

The use of such magical links in the termination phase must be analyzed and dealt with properly. Since they are now considered to be fully adult, the analyst does not wean them but conducts his analytical business until the last moment.

"Review dreams" (Glover 1955) usually occur at this point as an indication to the patient that he can integrate opposing representations (Volkan 1976). What remains for him is to express genuine affection for and gratitude to his analyst as well as sadness over the end of their very long association.

After termination is effected, mourning is likely to continue until resolution. As Bird (1972) suggests, some patients cannot fully appreciate the reality of termination until after it takes place, and I believe that patients who undertake treatment in a severely regressed and/or undeveloped state usually fall into this category. The account of my work with Pattie, which appears in Part II, is designed to make the six steps described here come to life.

PART II

Chapter 6

Pattie: A Psychosis-Prone Borderline Patient

DIAGNOSTIC PROFILE

Pattie was 21 when she came to my office for the diagnostic interview that was to lead to six years and seven months in treatment. Although she lived about a hundred miles from my office, she came four times a week until, during her last two years of treatment, her added job responsibilities made it necessary to reduce her time with me to three weekly visits.

When I first saw her she wore a wrinkled shirt and cutoff jeans stained with dirt. She might have been considered pretty were it not for her aggressive expression. Her hair was uncombed, she was rather plump, and she walked with a masculine stride, holding her arms in a wrestler's defiant posture. Beneath her demeanor or fierce independence I sensed a frightened child asking for help.

She said that at age 14 she had been diagnosed as a schizophrenic and had presented so many problems at school that she had been sent to a school for the exceptional. She had seen a woman psychologist for therapy three times a week for four years before being admitted to a private hospital where she stayed for over two years, having therapy sessions with a woman psychoanalyst thrice weekly. When her hospitalization overtaxed her family's budget, she was discharged.

She and her family had heard of me through the psychoanalyst, whom I did not know, with whom I never spoke, and who seemed to have made little impression on Pattie, who seldom spoke of her during all our work together. She seemed not to have cathected to the lady analyst to any great extent. Pattie did report that during their face-to-face sessions this analyst had said very little, listening to her disclosures with eyes closed. Pattie retained a rather affectionate regard for her first therapist, however, feeling that she had tried to be helpful but had been handicapped by a lack of training. Pattie had lied to her psychoanalyst during her hospitalization, managing to keep from her an affair she was having with a troubled staff member, and the fact that toward the end of her hospital stay she had been pregnant and had undergone an abortion after being discharged.

Pattie's parents had bought a farm on which, besides the main house, was a cottage where there lived a young man and his wife who looked after the place and the few horses on it. Pattie's parents lived elsewhere, visiting the farm from time to time in expectation of moving there permanently after the father's retirement. Pattie went to this farm after she left the hospital; certain rooms in the main house were assigned to her, but it was understood that she enjoyed no ownership, and that she would get out whenever the family had houseguests. It was clear that she brought shame, anger, and frustration to her family, and that they were trying not to let her chaotic and eccentric lifestyle impinge on their orderly existence. I felt that she was perceived, in effect, as just another animal loose on the farm; apparently she also felt this, for she seldom slept in the house, preferring to bed down in the stable where she felt comfortable and could talk to the animals. On the few occasions when she did sleep in the house, she refused a bed, sleeping instead with her dog on a couch.

When she came to me she had been at the farm for more than a year, spending a great deal of time sleeping or dozing off. When she could afford it, she took drugs, and she went nightly to a nearby bar to pick up a stranger to bring home for a one-night stand, during which she experienced no orgasm. Many of these partners were truckdrivers. Once the sex act was over, she would perceive her partner as threatening and evil and would become aggressive. Since she acknowledged that there were often fights, I felt that she was frequently in physical danger. It was her habit to return to the stables once her partner for the night had made his departure.

I noted that, in general, Pattie had psychic boundaries—she knew where she ended and others began. Her boundaries seemed, however, to be full of holes in spite of having two appropriately distinct surfaces on which these holes appeared. When under the influence of drugs and at such moments as she experienced intense need for nurturing objects, she merged with objects in the environment. She described inconsistent patterns of behavior and opposing aspects of an unintegrated sense of self, usually referring to herself as "a big bad blob." She had enough vanity, however, to feel that were she to take pains with her appearance, she would be a veritable femme fatale.

Her images of other people ranged from one extreme to the other; a "good" truckdriver, for example, would suddenly become "a bad man." She described her parents as though they were fragmented. She was at a loss to describe the therapists she had had as total, integrated persons, and this was especially true of the psychoanalyst in the hospital. In respect to whatever was emotionally and symbolically rather neutral, her reality testing seemed unimpaired, but anything suggestive of psychic or physical intimacy made her so anxious that it blurred her perception of reality. She clung to aspects of her childhood omnipotence in order to deny danger; when she found herself with men who were drunk and armed with knives and pistols she chose to be oblivious to what was going on. When her omnipotence was threatened she used even more massive denial of the dangerous world. This maneuver seemed to account for her spending so much time during the day sleeping.

Her real world was frustrating; indeed, she was playing a role in keeping it so. I sensed that she was creating and controlling something traumatic but familiar, and I recalled Giovacchini's remarks (1967) about how, to persons with character disorders, "The environment has to be constructed so that their total ego organization is maintained" (p. 579). (See also Jacobson 1964.) I thought also that the dangerous environment was a reservoir for Pattie's externalized and unacceptable self- and object images and her projected untamed impulses and her defenses against them. I began at once to check the accuracy of this conclusion.

She knew she was a woman, but her desire to be male was strong enough to suggest during her diagnostic interviews that she was not unlike the female borderline transsexuals I worked with at one time (Volkan 1974, 1980b, Volkan and Berent 1976, Kavanaugh and Volkan 1978). Indeed, from time to time she had given thought to having transsexual surgery but had never been obsessed by this possibility. The female transsexual typically has a troubled, usually depressed, mother whom as a child she had wanted to rescue from her depression for selfish reasons, clinging to and exaggerating her fantasy of having a penis. It is as though, were the little girl to have a penis, she could offer it to her mother, making her sufficiently happy to provide good mothering; but since mothering is frustrating, the little girl's fantasied penis is not always a loving one but is contaminated with derivatives of aggression. Having a penis differentiates the child from the depressed mother, who has none, and in this way, the possession of a penis is a defense against fusion with a bad mother.

In adolescence, after the oedipal father rejects his daughter, failing to disentangle her from her troubled relationship with her mother, the female transsexual feels her entitlement to an aggressive penis crystallize. Pattie had longed for a penis in adolescence, wanting it not for lovemaking but as a tool of aggression with which to protect herself from the dangers inherent in object relations. She reported that at age 11 or 12 she had tried to stab her mother with a kitchen knife as she lay in bed. The penis she wanted was like a kitchen knife.

As a small girl she had glimpsed the vagina of her menstruating mother and now thought of her own as ugly and dirty. I sensed that her desire to have a penis was, over and above the castration issues of a higher level, in the service of differentiating herself from her mother and thus protecting herself from a push toward engulfment by her (Socarides 1978). Even while presenting herself as a tough veteran of life, Pattie managed to tell me that she knew she was "in a mess" and that she often thought of suicide.

It took three diagnostic sessions for me to understand some of the basic reasons for Pattie's illness. I wanted to have a map, not too detailed at first, to give me some idea of where we would go if we decided to travel together in treatment.

In giving my formulation of her psychological problems, I calculatedly include here some information that was not available to me during these first three hours; her story and its meaning unfolded slowly over the years we were together, but to give the reader a comprehensive picture I include some later findings. Pattie came from an apparently prosperous family. Her father was co-owner of a textile plant, and her mother, a housewife, was involved in charitable and community affairs and had an active social life among "the people who count." Their oldest child was a girl five years Pattie's senior; their second, a boy, was four years older than Pattie. When she was two and a half, another sister, Mary, was added to the family. Although the latter developed normally over time, she had orthopedic problems as a child and had had to wear leg braces.

Pattie made it clear that Mary's lameness had injured their mother's self-esteem, and that the mother had devoted herself to Mary at Pattie's expense. Mary had had difficulty achieving separation–individuation from this solicitous mother, and it seemed to Pattie that she had so clung to her that Pattie herself was pushed aside. Thus she, too, experienced separation–individuation problems. Pattie remembered being quieted by a pacifier until she was about four and recalled the envy and rage she had felt over having to take second place.

One day her mother struck a bargain with Pattie: she would get her a doll she wanted if she would give up her pacifier. To her surprise, her mother sealed the bargain by cutting up the pacifier when Pattie surrendered it; having believed that she could have both the doll and the pacifier, the child felt disillusioned. Later, while still a small child, she shoplifted a plastic baby bottle with which at one time she tried to nurse some baby rats, but which she used primarily as a replacement for the lost pacifier. It became a childhood fetish with which she could deal with her separation anxiety and even with transitional issues (Winnicott 1953). She could not part with it, and even as an adult she took it to the farm with her. When her pacifier was destroyed, she began having a repeated dream, which continually appeared during her treatment until its meaning was analyzed and, what was more important, until she developed more mature ego functions to deal with the issues in her dream. In this dream she had plastic-like chewing gum in her mouth and was unable to chew it; it stuck in her teeth, and she could neither swallow it nor spit it out. She would then awaken with anxiety. Her oral fixation was represented in this dream. Greatly desiring her mother's love (her breast), she dreaded the possibility that what she longed for might turn sour. Not only did her mother's preoccupation with Mary make her "bad," but Pattie's projections of her aggression onto her mother made her dangerous.

The perpetual chewing reflected Pattie's state of limbo in respect to her relationship with her mother, whose satellite she had become. The *satellite state* (Volkan and Corney 1968) occurs in maladaptation to separation–individuation difficulties; a person in this state is drawn to the mother's representation as a moth is drawn to a flame. Closeness (a pull toward fusion with the representation of the mother) creates danger, while distancing (individuation) brings loneliness for which the individual in question is unprepared. The end result is that he is doomed to circle around the mother or her representation.

Patients like Pattie usually stay near the parental home as young adults and alternate between closeness and distance in respect to the mothering person. Both parties to this peculiar attraction act in the real world as though they are endlessly involved in the separation–individuation process. In this sense the child and the mother, caught in a developmental struggle, are kept alive (reactivated daily) without any result.

Pattie's childhood habit of biting her playmates, and her early preoccupation with such images as that of "Pac-Man," the devouring moveable mouth of the electronic game, directly expressed her oral sadism, which would be condensed later with anal and phallic sadistic impulses. She made a point of telling me that the knife with which she had tried to kill her mother (a phallic symbol) had "teeth," by which she no doubt meant that it had a serrated edge; in this remark one could sense the condensation of phallic and oral aggression.

When at first I learned during the diagnostic interviews about Pattie's mother having a disabled child for whom she had neglected Pattie, I had wondered whether this neglect alone could account for Pattie's psychopathological state. I could see no specific traumatic event save the destruction of the pacifier, but slowly I grasped that emotional poisons pervaded her family. She kept telling me that in spite of an outwardly stable appearance, her family was inwardly chaotic. As time went on I learned that the mother was fragile and had held second place with her tyrannical father, and she feared him even as an adult.

Pattie felt that her mother could function as a mother with only one child at a time and called her "The British Empire" because of something I said about the British maneuver of "divide and conquer." The sibling rivalry the mother had experienced was reflected in her own brood, and she could not face or control the sadistic competition among her own children. All of her children had problems. Her oldest daughter, who married a lawyer before Pattie became my patient, was her mother's extension, a favorite who had identified with her mother's rather narcissistic view of life. She was sadistic toward Pattie, whom she despised. Their brother struggled with obesity, and Mary had such separation anxiety that she too went into treatment.

The basic trauma Pattie had suffered at her mother's hands was not simply concerned with the destruction of the pacifier. We came to realize that the mother was deficient in certain ego functions such as the taming of affects, the integration of opposing elements, and some areas of reality testing in addition to being unable to help her children handle their rivalry. Pattie had not realized this until her own treatment progressed, and insight came to her suddenly after long preparation in therapy. When, with her father and a farmhand, Pattie was driving cattle one day into a corral, she saw her mother, dressed in street clothes, standing in the gateway of the corral, seemingly oblivious to the fact that she was obstructing the efforts of the others to get the cattle inside. Pattie had a flash of recognition that this was the story of her childhood—having to silently deal with having her mother not only fail to appreciate her efforts but to have any idea of their meaning.

Once Pattie cut down a dead tree in front of the living room window in the farmhouse and was angrily reproached by her mother, who claimed that she had wanted to see her grandchildren climb on it. She knew that the tree was dead but failed to take that into account. By now Pattie was able to see, as she had not been able to do before her treatment, that her mother's behavior was not always rational.

Frustrated by her mother, Pattie had turned to her father, who had initially been warmly responsive to her. When she was 8, however, he was bypassed for a political appointment he coveted; she could recall his getting the news and becoming deeply depressed. His depression activated his complicated mourning over the earlier death of an army comrade of whom he had been very fond, and his manner toward Pattie then became rather cynical and rejecting. He remained depressive for the rest of his life. Her father's rejection dealt a severe blow to Pattie's blossoming femininity; she seemed to change overnight into the "big bad blob," but she tried at first to find other support for her self-esteem by idealizing a woman teacher, thus returning to the possibility of finding a good mother. Soon, however, this teacher became pregnant and left school, leaving Pattie rejected once again, by a mother figure who, like Pattie's own mother, gave attention to a new baby. Her history had repeated itself! She reacted by shoplifting again, in a sense making a store an instant gratifier (Volkan 1976), taking a lipstick from a shop with which her father had a business connection. Rejected by a mother substitute, she envisioned getting her father's attention by using the lipstick she had taken and showing that she was now a grown woman. She had once had high hopes of being his favorite. But the theft of the lipstick led to her detention by the shopkeeper. Her mother was summoned and expressed anger at her daughter, and overnight Pattie again became "a big bad blob." When shown a picture of herself taken before she was 8, Pattie did not feel as though it was she. It seemed that being rejected by the teacher she idealized had been destructive, and now her failed attempt to protect her self-esteem was the last straw. She experienced a kind of organismic panic (Pao 1979), or emotional flooding (Volkan 1976).

Her ego functions returned and she began to establish the best possible sense of self. She emerged from this experience with a personality change. Although Pattie did not go into a full-blown psychosis, she seemed to break out of her helplessness, finding support for her self-esteem and reorganizing a new self. This occurred through crystallization of her "big bad blob" identity, which led her to think of herself as someone other than the child in the photograph. Her newly crystallized "bad" self did not, however, overcome her hopeful "good" self but put it in abeyance; it was better to have daily a "bad" self and a split off, hidden "good" self than to have no self at all. In order to support the "bad" self she tried to maintain, she began to play "games of being bad," which were, paradoxically, the only way to get her mother's attention and to identify with her crippled little sister, who in her mind, was bad. The games led her to break implicit family rules to respect what belonged to her siblings; to assume a tough, mean, masculine identity; and to split away from and hide her gentle and femininely seductive aspects. Although at one time she had shown affection for Mary, she soon came to feel rejected by her and added this supposed rejection to her reasons for being "a big bad blob."

She forgot how to smile when she was eight, and she began wanting to be a boy, although there remained a hidden desire to save her father from his depression (condensed with her earlier savior fantasy about her mother) and a hope that some day she would regain his appreciation and love. Now her expectations of him were hidden behind constant bickering with him. As long as she fought with him she could hide her desire for his love; it was as though she felt that he would be nice to her if they stopped fighting but she was afraid to put this to a test for fear of being disappointed and so kept on being belligerent. Thus she kept the possibility of being either loved or rejected by her father in limbo just as she kept closeness and distance from her mother.

Much later she realized through her dreams that the truck-drivers she picked up represented not only the nipple that had solaced her as a child and her "good" mother but also the "good" (saved) father. All of these consolations could suddenly cease to comfort—or even to be acceptable. By the time she was an adolescent she had become expert in finding reasons for her aggression toward and mistrust of others, and it was through such primitive mechanisms as splitting, denial, externalization, and projection she could so readily create a hostile environment. In all truth, the environment of her real world—her treatment at the hands of her older sister, for example—was hostile enough to be congruent with her pathological expectations. Unable to form mature relationships within her peer group, she suffered in mid- and late adolescence from massive identity diffusion, feeling alienated from other girls and boys. The world became dangerous in her view, and she tried to kill her mother.

Her parents sent her to a summer riding camp, where the discipline of riding well was beyond her. Feeling great anxiety, she withdrew more and more from people and began talking to the horses and hearing messages in the wind. It was soon after this that she began her first treatment with the psychologist.

After six years in treatment with two therapists, and after more than a year on the farm, Pattie came to me. Although consulting me had been discussed with her parents, I think it was the "accidental" killing of a kitten that precipitated her to visit my office. In panic she came for treatment. The death had made her very anxious, and in treatment I came to believe that it was an actualization of her unconscious fantasy of killing her younger sister.

PHENOMENOLOGICAL DIAGNOSIS

As a psychoanalyst I am more interested in making a psychological profile of my patient, and a detailed formulation of his psychodynamic processes and their psychogenetic determinants, than I am in making a diagnosis in a phenomenological sense. Here, however, I do diagnose in phenomenological terms according to DSM III (The Diagnostic and Statistical Manual of the American Psychiatric Association); such specificity is required now in order to qualify a patient for third-party underwriting in treatment. DSM III lists eight personality-trait determinants in diagnosing Borderline Personality Organization, in which five are required for a positive diagnosis. In terms of the DSM III, I saw Pattie as suffering from Borderline Personality Disorder (DSM III, pp. 322–323); she exhibited *all eight* of the determinants of this diagnosis:

1. She was impulsive and unpredictable in such matters as substance abuse, stealing, and overeating—aspects of potential self-destruction.

2. She seemed unable to control anger, appearing to be at times in the grip of murderous rage and at other times chronically angry.

3. Her interpersonal relationships were marked by attitudinal shifts involving both idealization and devaluation.

4. She had disturbance of identity, seeming uncertain about her gender identity and her body image.

5. She had affective instability, being easily moved by either internal or external stimuli to anxiety, depression, and irritability. These affective states would run their course in a matter of hours, after which time she would present herself in a normal mood.

6. She could not tolerate being alone. When there was no one around she retreated into long hours of sleep or talked to the animals. Then she would frantically seek out people like the truckdrivers, none of whom became friends.

7. She behaved in ways that jeopardized her physical well-being, although she had never attempted suicide in spite of thinking about it from time to time. On occasion she got into physical struggles with a truckdriver, just as she had fought physically with her siblings and other children when a youngster. When she slept in the stable she exposed herself to injury, and had in fact been kicked and bitten by the animals.

8. She felt chronically empty and reported being bored and dissatisfied in spite of her alternating periods of dangerous activity and sleep.

Pattie had all eight of the characteristics of Borderline Personality Disorder to a marked degree. Her anger became murderous, she displayed transient symptoms of psychosis, and she could not maintain, even with her parents, the kind of relationship with others that would offer protection. I felt that her Borderline Personality Disorder was on the lowest level. Her shifts from one extreme of affect and attitude to another, and her frantic activities punctuated a customary state of being from which she operated from day to day; it was not a loving or idealized state, but one invested with hate in which she had an aggressively weighted self-concept and considered herself "a big bad blob." Phenomenologically at least, her condition might be like Narcissistic Personality Disorder, which implies the day-to-day domination of the clinical picture by a "stable state of mind" in spite of a grandiose sense of self-importance and preoccupation with success, power, beauty, or ideal love. Unable to organize herself at this level, Pattie went to the opposite level; to her, a bad and negative identity was better than none at all. However, like a narcissistic person, she wanted to be "Number One" and tried in her customary state to be the worst person on earth, although her exaggeratedly bad stance and sense of self-devaluation were less stable than were she of the narcissistic type, which stoutly maintains its inflated self-importance.

DECISION FOR TREATMENT

I did not see Pattie as a candidate for unmodified traditional psychoanalysis, which is designed basically to treat those who are neurotic and who have a high-level personality organization or high-level borderline personality organization. All indications pointed to her being very likely to exhibit transference psychosis, with acting out that could be dangerous to herself and others. During her stay in the hospital earlier, her analyst had probably tried the classical psychoanalytic approach, listening rather passively during their sessions to whatever Pattie had to say. Indeed, Pattie claimed that her analyst had made but few remarks during their two years of work together. During her four previous years in supportive therapy with a psychologist, she had received help in having some of her dangerous activities curtailed by the cultivation of a positive transference (which was never analyzed, nor was the negative transference), by consultation with her parents, and so forth. Such efforts had not been enough, however.

She was at a point where it seemed advisable to take a chance on using an undiluted version of psychoanalytic therapy that I had already tried with other psychosis-prone borderline patients, usually with success. I thought that if we did not take this chance, her life would be in danger, whether from a knife at the hand of one of her truckdrivers, the kick of a horse, or injudicious use of drugs. Or she might wind up having to be repeatedly hospitalized, with someone to manage her life most of the time.

Arrangement to Pay for Treatment

I told Pattie that I would work with her and see her four times a week. I expressed some concern about her willingness to drive this often from a hundred miles away, but she replied that she did not mind driving and had been in any case thinking of moving to the city in which I work. During her final diagnostic session she reported that her parents wanted to meet with me. I told her I preferred having our work remain a matter between the two of us. Her father wanted to know the yearly cost of her projected treatment, and I came up with a figure allowing for the usual two months or so of my absence for academic meetings and holidays. I said that my academic duties made me somewhat less readily available than the average psychoanalyst in private practice.

Pattie was the beneficiary of a trust fund, but her father managed her income because she was thought to be sick. I suggested that she make her own financial arrangements with him about paying for her treatment and bring me checks she had signed herself. I explained our system of professional reimbursement in the Medical Center but stressed that her bringing in payment for her bills herself would be an acknowledgment of her responsibility for her treatment. Later, when she began earning, she was able to shoulder this responsibility directly without consultation with her father.

Instructions

I told her that I did not give medication, and that we would work by her telling me whatever came into her mind and acquainting me with her bodily sensations during sessions. I also said I expected her to use the couch soon after we started. I told her that using the couch was productive, and my not being visible to her would, in the long run, help her to let her mind wander more freely. Also, it might make it easier for her to share and examine her fantasies about me and the treatment. Examination of such fantasies would be essential. A veteran of therapeutic work, Pattie knew about the customary use of the couch in psychoanalysis although she had not used one herself. I explained that it would be through free associations and reports of her bodily sensations that we would try to grasp how her mind worked and why it functioned as it did; thus in time she would come to see choices available to her in relation to her lifestyle, her relationships to others, and, most importantly, to herself.

She understood my instructions and expressed satisfaction in my refusing to meet her parents. She said she felt that I was taking my work with her very seriously.

Chapter 7

Step One: The Establishment of a Reality Base

ON THE COUCH

A month after the diagnostic interviews, we commenced our work. Pattie took an apartment near my office but continued going to the farm on weekends, and occasionally during the week, to see the animals.

She tried at first to tell me more of her history, but I saw that her mind focused on the couch. She was anxious that as a Freudian I might reenforce her perception that Freud was against women. She tried to set conditions for her agreeing to use the couch; I must, for example, refrain from speaking of issues such as penis envy. My response was designed to develop a working alliance without my abandoning my therapeutic neutrality. I asked her to grant me freedom to tell her whatever I might consider useful, stating that she need not agree with anything I said that made no sense to her. We had already, at the end of her diagnostic interviews, discussed her use of the couch, but when she began to bargain I did not remind her of our original agreement.

I heard no protest when I asked her to start lying on the couch during the second week of the four-times-a-week schedule we established. She did complain, however, that the design of the fabric on my couch reminded her of open mouths, and I sensed that she was thinking of the possibility of my biting or eating her (to have her self-representation merge with me, to be symbiotic with me) and her dread of this. I surmised that this was a clue to one of her basic dilemmas that would take much time to work through in treatment. I did not interpret her comment but had her realize that I recognized her anxiety over a new way of working in treatment and her hesitation to embark on a close working relationship.

On her first day on the couch she brought a soft drink, taking a deep swallow from it before lying down and leaving the bottle half empty on the floor by the couch. I said nothing, knowing that the bottle was a safety valve, something that she could reach for instead of bravely submitting herself to the opening of a possibly devouring mouth. I refrained from expressing my admiration for her courage, and there was no bottle on the following day.

During her first hours on the couch, Pattie complained about her parents, explained how she could not deny her impulse to have sex with strangers, and gave some details of the abortion she had had under trying conditions and that she had kept secret from her parents.

The First Dream

The first dream Pattie reported was about being in a kitchen with a gray-haired man who it appeared represented myself. She was cooking a meal with him that looked like spaghetti cooked in blood, with meatballs like lumps of uncooked meat. When the food was spooned onto plates, Pattie began carrying the plates to the table but dropped them on the floor, making what looked like a bloody mess. The man insisted that it was her mess, one she was responsible for cleaning up. She felt angry and frustrated and awakened with anxiety.

She began to associate spontaneously to this dream like a

veteran of therapeutic inquiry. Among other things, she spoke of the fetus she had aborted, which she thought was represented by the blood and raw meat in her dream, and of having as a child seen her mother's menstruation. Although her associations seemed valid, I felt that a display of interest would take us on a wild goose chase. When she spoke of the man with gray hair as my representative, I said I could understand her frustration and anger if she thought I would require her to do difficult chores without an understanding of her ability to do them and offering no help. My aim during the opening hours of treatment is to set the stage for the formation of a core of therapeutic alliance.

She was grossly untidy and had a bad smell when she came to her sessions, and her dress fitted her description of herself as "a big bad blob": her slacks were bloody because, she claimed, she was without money for tampax, she spoke of having a girlfriend she saw from time to time who had fleas and lice and claimed she had become infested with them herself. She spoke of her skin being greasy but showed no concern about soiling my couch or walking on my carpet with muddy shoes.

I thought that her physical nastiness was related to the mess on the floor in her dream, and that she was responding to my offer to help her clean it up, having a desire to cleanse herself inwardly. I said nothing about this but made remarks that I felt would promote the building of a working relationship. She came in one day with a deep gash on her arm that she had suffered while working on her car. It was surrounded with both fresh and dried blood, and when she flourished it at me defiantly I told her that I saw her as a girl wounded in more than one way, and that she could in her own good time disclose her psychological wounds verbally rather than bodily. I knew as a physician that a wound badly cared for could very well become infected and asked her if she would consider keeping the wound on her arm clean or get it taken care of. Wouldn't it be better for us to continue our psychotherapeutic work without such an obstacle as an infected arm?

Conflicting Inner Voices

She responded with a lovely, friendly smile I had not supposed her capable of. Then she laughed nervously and said that she was a veteran of many wars. It was after this exchange that she told me of her two conflicting "inner voices" in her head. One voice, which she referred to as "the pain in the ass," harshly gave her orders about almost anything. It might tell her, "You are late waking up! Get up now!" The other voice would object, saying, "Don't listen to that creep!" The first voice would advise perfection, the second was rebellious. I noted unintegrated and unassimilated self- and object representations and a struggle between the superego forerunners and her impulses.

Conflicting Self-Images

In spite of her physically appearing in my office as the "big bad blob," I learned very early in her treatment that she often had fantasies about being a movie star when she was behind the wheel of her car. However, she could not tolerate maintaining an idealized image of herself; after having such fantasies she often put herself in a position to be hurt, as when she allowed herself to be stung by a bee. It occurred to me that she hoped that by my seeing her as glamorous, I would like her, as a father would like a daughter. But since she expected to be rejected by me as she had been rejected by her father, she would quickly assume a masochistic identity. I thought that in exposing herself to the sting of a bee there was a sexual reference. She desired her father but punished herself with pain!

I think it is a technical mistake with a patient like Pattie to plunge into investigation, clarification, or interpretation of psychosexual issues; an analyst lets his mind wander while listening to a patient, and I report here what kinds of thoughts came to me that I refrained from commenting on as I listened to Pattie. It seemed better to help her develop a therapeutic alliance and start establishing a work ego.

She often dreamed of ruined houses and of a child she referred to as "a Biafran kid," having heard of starvation in Biafra. This child was trying to escape danger with the only means available to him—a small child's scooter. I thought this child, with his inadequate means of escape, represented Pattie herself.

She spoke of my being "awesome," and after telling about

going to her school prom inappropriately dressed and suffering ridicule for it, she came to her session in an absurd outfit about which I refrained from comment; she wanted to see if I would ridicule her and any explanation would acknowledge her dress as being ridiculous, and this would hurt her. I am rather chary of this type of explanation in this phase of treatment, trying to develop overall treatment plans rather than stopping to particularize.

Externalization as a Transference Manifestation

As time went on, it became clear that a transference configuration was evolving; she was trying to use me as a reservoir of her bad aspects and feelings. This was the first clear indication that my representation was becoming involved in her expected introjective-projective relatedness. In fact, she verbalized this when she recalled her first dream a month and a half after first reporting it. "The blood in the dream has something to do with my fantasies," she said, noting to the effect that if she bled copiously, evil within her would magically spill out with her blood. "Now," she added, "I really want to give you all this shit and make you clean it up. I want to be free of it!" She said in a harsh masculine voice, "Don't hang out your dirty laundry!" When I asked what she meant, she said that what I had heard was her first inner voice giving an order to her. She knew that the voice came from an assimilated inner father image.

I said that if there were any way for me to take what troubled her away and to clean up her mess, we might consider it, but since opposing suggestions in her mind were expressed by her inner voices, it was clear that we would have to work together to bring about any improvement. I again spoke in a way that suggested the necessity of a working alliance.

INITIAL REACTIONS OF THE ANALYST

Once when Pattie fell asleep on the couch, snoring for at least half an hour, I relaxed in my chair and made no effort to rouse her before the end of the session. I told her that while I listened to the sounds she made I had been trying to account for her falling asleep and what I felt about this. I told her I did not really know why she had fallen asleep, but I felt comfortable knowing that she trusted me enough to sleep on my couch. On the following day she once more fell asleep briefly on the couch, awakening spontaneously after ten minutes. (She did not fall asleep again until she was in the third step and later in the termination phase when she was reviewing her initial symptoms.) However, she often overslept at home so as to miss her hour with me or be late for it. She seemed to use sleep for different purposes. Her sleep on the couch was, I felt, the sleep of a child after a hard day, defensive but at the same time evidence of trust in me. I enjoyed in a motherly way watching her sleep; a deep psychological relationship was growing between us.

The Analyst's Temporary Identification with the Patient

Three months after our work began I noticed my bodily reaction to her pent-up anger when I temporarily identified with her, discovering how it was to have such feelings within oneself. This came about in connection with her relationship with a young man working on the farm who had been the target of her aggression since the start of treatment. Apparently she was pleasant enough to him when they were face to face, but she would tell me on the couch how bad he was, how he was a lazy, obnoxious freeloader. Sometimes the harsh inner voice that strove to make her perfect would address him in a peculiar, masculine way from the couch. I came to believe that he and his wife represented to Pattie her unloved siblings. I kept this observation to myself. At times her anger was vicious, and I know she would not "hear" any interpretation about how the pair represented her siblings. Moreover, any interference of mine with the "transference" outside our relationship would be seen by her as my taking sides.

One day she was greatly frustrated because she could not speak out in anger toward the couple who she said had done something wrong on the farm. As she spoke about her pent-up anger I suddenly felt nauseated. I realized I was identifying with her when she pointed to her stomach and said that this was where she usually felt her emotions. I think, however, that I was also identifying with Pattie's "victims," the targets of her anger. She told me that she had uncontrollably attacked her siblings and their mother. "Once I hit them," she said, "I would have no mercy!" I said nothing to her about my nausea and remained silent. As if sensing my "fear," she added, "I never beat up anybody except members of my family, some classmates, and my lover [the staff member of the hospital where she had been confined who made her pregnant]." She was telling me not to be afraid of her anger. My feeling of nausea disappeared at once, but through my temporary identification with her and her victims I experienced the effects of her aggression. Although she finally caused the discharge of the farm couple who so angered her, their successors met a similar fate.

The Patient's Perception of the Analyst as a Collaborator

On the day after I had felt nauseated I felt that she perceived me as her collaborator in being aggressive toward a dangerous world; both of us would be "big bad blobs" in order to keep others at a distance and, if need be, to victimize them. She was now able to speak openly of her murderous fantasies. She announced that my accent indicated that I was a German. Since I had never mentioned my ethnic origin, I could not regard this as a misperception and did not correct her. She went on to describe how she identified with Hitler, "a twisted genius." A child of Christian parents, at no time did she report anti-Semitism on their part; in her remarks about Hitler, she was externalizing her own images on Hitler. She let me know that she still could control her aggression, saying that although she would beat up her enemies, but, unlike the Nazis, she would not kill them. I recalled, however, her story of attacking her mother with a knife, and I was not so confident in her ability to control her anger sufficiently to avoid doing harm to others.

I was involved in her introjective-projective cycle, reacting to it and, in the long run, tolerating it. I experienced temporary identification with her and with the representations of her introjects (her victims). It seemed that our psychological work together had begun, and that we were set to travel in an intrapsychic world. With this understanding, I felt that the first step of her treatment had concluded.

Chapter 8

Step Two: The First Split Transference

HOW TO *NOT* MANAGE THE PATIENT'S LIFE

It is hard to summarize the second step in Pattie's treatment. It was chaotic and lasted for two years. Even during those hours when she was organized, and our treatment seemed routine, she externalized on me various fragments of her unmended self-representations and unmended object representations. She had many perceptions of me: as Hitler, as a money-grabber, as the woman-hating Freud, as someone "awesome," or as the only person she could talk to. She held onto the idea of herself as "a big bad blob" by continuing to wear clothing stained with barnyard dirt, although on occasion she came in as a femme fatale, wearing a red blouse and red shoes, with dark red lipstick on her lips. Then she looked pathetic, and like a streetwalker. Sometimes she tried bolder seduction, wearing a low-cut blouse and exposing her legs.

I saw these occasions as a replay of her having alienated her father by growing into obvious sexuality. Her attempts to display herself, which were not unconscious, were short-lived. I saw that on many occasions her playing the role of a femme fatale was in the service of the "upward resistance" I have described. I could see many transference manifestations, but they could not be worked through systematically since they were not sustained long enough.

She responded to any physical separation between us by more frantically searching for strangers with whom to have sexual intercourse. I tried to show her how she was reacting to my occasional cancellation of an hour with her, but although she could understand the mechanics of the matter, she could not assimilate what she took in. The next time I cancelled an hour she found another truckdriver. When at last she gave up her one-night stands, she started spending time with emotionally disturbed young men. She had an occasional relationship with the man who had made her pregnant, and they would be lovers for a week or so, after which he would disappear. He took her to a beach near his home in the North, where, accustomed to icy water, he expected her to swim as he did. This precipitated a quarrel, with acrimonious reference to the Civil War. He held her head under water until she almost drowned, and this led her to refuse him when he asked to see her again. He promptly married someone else.

Seeing a patient leading such a chaotic life, an analyst may think it necessary to manage the patient. I knew, however, that if I did this with Pattie, there would be no end to it. I would become a parent and thus lose the opportunity for intrapsychic work with her. Accordingly, I did nothing to alter her lifestyle except when her activities seemed to interfere with her session, in which case I would voice my concern. For example, when she spoke of wanting to take an impulsive trip with a boyfriend that would necessitate cancelling a session with me, I would say, very directly, that I felt nothing was more important than her keeping her appointment with me.

LINKING INTERPRETATIONS

During hours with Pattie when everything seemed calm I made linking interpretations (Giovacchini 1969). Without using technical terms, I tried to verbalize with her the way she was using splitting and introjective-projective relatedness and other primitive defense mechanisms, and how evidence of their use appeared in her everyday life. For example, when Pattie said that the dead leaves on a plant in my office indicated that I was a poor caretaker, willing to withhold water and nourishment, I sensed that she identified with the plant and feared my rejection. On the day after this exchange she reported stealing food from her roommate, whom she had found by advertising and to whom she related as though she were a dangerous sibling. I *linked* her theft of food with her remarks about my failing to feed the plant in my office. I told her that the plant was a symbol of her needy aspect, that since she felt I was not taking care of it she was entitled to her roommate's food. I was careful in explaining her action but mentioned no prohibition or anything that could induce guilt in her. I tried to approach her from the side of the ego (explaining reasons, linking two events, etc.) rather than from the side of the superego (with prohibitions, fault-finding, etc.). I did not tell her that in taking food from her roommate she was reliving her mother's having Mary and making Pattie feel rejected, although she herself rather pointed to a connection. Connections with genetic issues were not emotionally hot; knowing about them did not in any case keep Pattie from repeating them in the here-and-now. Her problem was not a lack of knowledge about her childhood but a difficulty in integrating the past with the present. When psychogenetic aspects were hot—as, for example, when she recalled a childhood memory with overwhelming affect—my trying to connect this memory with some current activity would be seen by her as evidence that I lacked empathy. In such circumstances I felt it best to absorb her emotions by making empathic sounds or by remaining silent.

She reported chaotic dreams, most indicating paranoid fears of entrapment and depicting ruins that represented her low self-esteem, her body image, and her identification with the sister who was crippled. I was most interested in finding connections between her dreams and their day residue since they can provide another illustration of the linking interpretations made, and prepare the patient to be curious but not fearful about psychological processes and connections to be found at deeper levels. For example, at the beginning of one month Pattie "forgot" to bring her check and dreamt that night that she was babysitting for her cousin's children. When the cousin and his wife came home, they were intoxicated and the children were still running around. When her cousin told Pattie to stay longer and continue caring for the children, she retorted, "But you haven't paid me yet!"

I stressed the link between her forgetfulness about paying me and her cousin's about paying her. The notion of such links usually delighted Pattie and she soon tried to discover some herself, thus becoming better able to free-associate in an effective way instead of coming up with a caricature of free association. For example, when I returned from a meeting after an absence of three days, she reported a dream in which she was trying to escape from an institution. In it she met a man who offered to help her and carry her on his shoulders. She rubbed her legs as though massaging his back, and he enjoyed this. Since there were killings in the institution from which she sought to escape, she needed his help desperately, but suddenly realized that he was an impostor. At this point she awakened with anxiety. In telling me this dream she spontaneously said that I was the man in the dream and that she had thought of my being an impostor because I had left her and canceled two sessions. She said that she was disappointed in me. She made no attempt to understand the dream's latent content, and I did not push her. I was delighted, however, when she reported another linking interpretation: On the way to my office she had had a fantasy in which the couple recently discharged from the farm might return to the farm and injure her. She now connected this fantasy with her anger at me for my absence and with her expectation of punishment.

A TEMPORARY RETURN TO STEP ONE

I had agreed, the reader will recall, to work with Pattie without talking to her parents. In view of how hard it was for her to control her aggressive impulses, however, I was so alarmed to hear that her father had given her a rifle with which he had taught her to shoot groundhogs that I debated sharing my alarm with her parents. After some thought, I decided not to and to follow the flow of her treatment without interference.

Three months after being given the gun, she tried to help a horse on the farm free a leg that had become wedged in the cattle guard. She thought that the horse would inevitably be lame but made no conscious connection between a horse with an injured leg and her sister Mary. When her efforts to free the horse proved unsuccessful, she rationalized that it must be shot, and killed it, after which she became disorganized to the point of picking up two strangers that night to have sex with. (I recalled that she had sought treatment with me after killing a kitten that, according to my formulation, represented her sister.)

At her session the following day I asked her to sit up, and we returned temporarily to Step One to help stop her disorganization by infusing just enough reality testing. Acknowledging that it might have been necessary to shoot the horse, I told her that the prospectively lame horse might have reminded her of the lame sister whose birth had robbed her of their mother's attention. If we slowed down we might seize the symbolic meaning of her shooting the horse. Again, I knew that it was not interpretation of the psychogenesis of the shooting that would be important, although it might be of some help, but my attitude opposing her disorganization. It was possible that I was demonstrating my professionalism in seeking the reason for her inner commotion and offering myself as "a mattress for her to fall on." I then made a new arrangement for our work, a kind of limit-setting, telling her to put the rifle away until we could work out the meaning of this incident.

This face-to-face session lasted about half an hour. She seemed to appreciate what I was saying about being better organized, and she lay on the couch once again. That night one of her casual sex partners gave her a puppy that I thought of as a substitute for the horse, and it helped relieve her feelings of unconscious guilt. Mary had returned to life! Although I expressed an interest in the puppy she described, I offered no interpretation of its meaning since doing so at this time would be like stripping the bandage off her wound, providing nothing to take its place. (A year later she shot another horse that had been in an accident that would have left it crippled. This time she was not disorganized, nor did she recall the first shooting and my comments about it, but she tried to prove that the shooting had been justified by real circumstances.)

THE INABILITY TO INTEGRATE THE PAST WITH THE PRESENT

Pattie's feeling of being rejected because of Mary's presence and her murderous feelings toward this sibling were a routine feature in her sessions. For example, when I left for a few days she fantasized that I was going to a convention where the correction of pigeon-toes would be discussed. Mary was pigeon-toed. I was the mother rejecting her to take care of Mary. She said she was very angry about my leaving her, but that she could not express her anger because if she did I or a pigeon-toed patient at the convention would die. Since none of this transference configuration persisted from session to session, she could not experience it in a therapeutically effective way. Even when I made interpretations, they were hit-and-run. Moreover, when she made an intellectual connection between a present and a past behavior pattern, she could not assimilate or make use of this intellectual understanding since her observing, integrating, and assimilating ego functions were not yet adequate. Nevertheless, the most important part of the treatment during Step Two was my providing her with a holding environment (Winnicott 1960, Modell 1976).

LIMIT SETTING

Besides telling her to put the rifle away for awhile, I set other limits in this phase of the treatment as she brought certain issues to her sessions. For example, she showed the effects of the splitting of her self-representations, being "all bad" one day and seductive the next. Without telling me, she made an appointment with a counselor for help with her heavy drinking. I thought that not only was she actively splitting herself, but she was splitting me, too, by having two therapists at the same time. I then set limits, telling her that one unintegrated person in the room was enough, and that her seeing a counselor while she was my patient was absolutely unacceptable. She then cancelled her appointment with the counselor, seemed more solemn than before, and made observations about how she went from one of her selves to the other. She would get very anxious while changing from having a good self to a bad self. Her anxiety vanished once she became the "big bad blob" (her bad self). I noted that her anxiety arose from the contest between her libidinally loaded self-representation and her aggressively loaded one. I explained her object relations conflict—her fear of losing her loved self if it were united with her hated self. It was easier for her to be all bad (black) than something in between (grey). Another example of limit-setting arose from her coming twice to my office while under the influence of drugs and alcohol; I told her I could not work with her under such circumstances and asked that she leave and come back when she was sober.

TAMING AGGRESSION

Pattie's attempt to tame her aggression by identifying with her analyst's protective functions appeared for the first time in a dream she reported during her first hour after a holiday separation. She had tolerated the separation rather well, and observed that she had tried to create me in others, only to realize that no one represented me, and that I, who took her seriously, was unique in her experience. She had dreamt of a harbor. She was in the water with some horses, which probably represented aspects of herself and her siblings. They were surrounded by a fence-like coral reef, which protected them from sharks. There was a break in the reef like a gate, and a man was in charge of it, letting boats in and out, but always shutting the gate against the sharks. I thought Pattie was describing the holding environment (a womb symbol) that her treatment was providing for her.

In her dream, the man disappeared (reflecting my absence

because of the holidays). She continued swimming but suddenly realized that without the man at the gate, the enclosure was now open and sharks (probably representing siblings contaminated with her oral aggression) could enter and devour her and the horses. She tried to close the gate the way the man had done; it had seemed easy for him, but it was too heavy for her. When at length she succeeded in closing the gate she felt happy.

When we resumed after the holidays Pattie was 20 pounds thinner and looked more feminine. She continued to dress sloppily, however, and to have one-night stands. (She would lose and gain weight throughout her treatment until the termination phase, during which she kept a good figure.) Her behavior no longer seemed so frantic, but she had had to have treatment for a venereal disease. She felt as though I offered no protection, and as though she were being attacked. She dreamt of being infested with lice and developed an intense negative transference. I made the interpretation that her having a venereal disease made her perceive me as uncaring. Soon, however, she went back to work with me instead of simply feeling paranoid in session after session. Sometimes she seemed close to me, but at other times she felt afraid of me. She would dream of herself, represented by an animal, being starved or devoured by rats. Sometimes she was afraid that the children she assumed I had would die. She thought of me as ill and asked, "Is there something the matter with you?"

I helped her to see the flow of her aggressive drive. She relived her childhood in primitive fantasies, but I provided limits to her drive expression, limits that she had not had in her childhood environment; I explained how her mind worked and facilitated her reality testing, becoming a catalyst for her development of new functions. I was not simply a caretaker.

A CRUCIAL JUNCTURE

Pattie had a memorable dream two years and two months after starting treatment. In it she was held captive in a house. A woman wearing what Pattie called an "S.M. uniform" (sadomasochism), meaning the Nazi S.S., had tied her to a table. While Pattie lay on her back the woman tore her body into two sections, which probably represented her split self-representation. A man entered, handcuffed the woman, and took her away. Before she left, the woman turned to Pattie and seemed to have had no idea that she had been hurting her. She said, "You know, I only wanted to love you and give you pleasure."

This dream disturbed Pattie. She told me with certainty that the woman in the dream was her mother. Since she was lying on a table in the dream as she lay on my couch, I also was the sadistic mother in the transference. But I was also the man who handcuffed the mother. What really surprised Pattie was her sudden insight that her mother's behavior toward her had never been part of a malign design, but an indication that her mother had not known how to love and mother her in proper fashion.

I noticed at our next session that Pattie had had her hair cut. She said that after the previous session she had remembered how her mother had tried to help her by attempting to cut her hair, but had only succeeded in pulling it and making her scalp hurt. This recollection led to her cutting her own hair, symbolically developing a function in which her mother was deficient. After succeeding in cutting her hair without hurting herself, Pattie decided to buy a feminine kind of hat, indicating a desire for a new type of identity organization.

A few days later she confided that she now understood that having sex was for her like taking a drug—it was an addiction. Her one-night stands continued, but they were less frequent since she had found some boyfriends. From this time to the end of her treatment, she picked up only two strangers, one in the third step and another in the termination phase when she was "revisiting" her old symptoms.

New Psychic Structure

Two years and four months into her treatment, with Christmas approaching, she talked about wanting to give me a white narcissus bulb for a Christmas gift. I was to pot it for my office, water it, and see it flower. I understood that, with her association to the S.S. woman of her dream, she was putting the aggressive mother and the loving mother image together, having arrived at the "crucial juncture" (Kernberg 1975) where integration of split object representations becomes possible. Accordingly, I thought that she would give birth to a new, integrated self-representation represented by the narcissus bulb, and that she wanted me to nurture it.

When at the crucial juncture where opposite self- and object units meet, with their corresponding affective states, a patient usually feels sad, experiencing a sense of loss, especially of all good representations. Pattie said, "I am feeling sad now, but now sadness does not lead to nothingness." She was comparing this new feeling with her childhood hopelessness and depression; sadness had been intolerable then.

I did not commit myself to accept her gift of the white narcissus, but encouraged her to talk about it inasmuch as its meaning seemed important. She gave up the idea of giving it to me, and, about this time she related a dream about a building. The walls of the ruined building still stood despite the gaps like the holes in Swiss cheese. Inside, the building was full of growing plants. After her dream, she reported experiencing a sense of calm and normalcy.

In reference to the start of new structures within herself, she declared, "Now everything is your responsibility!" I responded by saying that we still needed to work together, since she would be the one to choose the sort of "building" to construct. I knew that her second step was now completed.

Chapter 9

Step Three: Focalized Psychotic Transference Leading to Reactivated and Transference-Related Transitional Phenomena

WOMB FANTASY

It seemed that Pattie was moving toward a plateau, one with less frenzy and more organization, and was allowing herself more genuine insight into her dilemma. It has been my experience that about this time in treatment such patients usually offer a dramatic regressive (and delusional) story. Although there may be some attempt to go directly from Step Two to Step Four, if the analyst does not interfere the patient goes to Step Three.

I do not mean to suggest that Pattie offered nothing in her sessions to this point that indicated clear reality testing. When she was paranoid she saw me as dangerous, and at other times she seemed to believe that I would die if she did something. Such psychotic manifestations, however, came and went, being too transient to develop a life of their own. In Step Three, however, a regressive therapeutic story unfolded from session to session, a phenomenon of which I myself, through my counterreactions, became a part.

When she fell asleep on my couch she awakened to tell me that her dropping off at this time was connected with her desire to kill the "big bad blob" as well as the femme fatale. At her next session, instead of falling asleep she lost all sensation in her back as she lay on the couch. The absence of tactile sensation let her merge with my couch (with me) and at the same time I felt drowsy, with heavy eyelids, and we had a kind of symbiotic relatedness. From day to day she felt my couch turning into a pool of water, and I observed that she was symbolically experiencing her fantasy of being in my womb—or behaving as though she were. Her feeling of being in water was so strong that she opened her arms and legs as though staying afloat. She was mostly silent, and if she felt sleepy she would suddenly jerk her body and explain that she felt as though she were sinking; the jerking would bring her to the surface, where she could swim.

She compared the lines on my office wall made by concealed wires to blood vessels. The room was indeed a womb! She even verbalized feeling connected with me by an umbilical cord. I continued to experience fusion with her. This did not lead to anxiety in either of us, which was certainly odd, but rather comfortable. It persisted for two weeks, and later, when less intense, it still made me feel that we were interchangeable. I felt that I had become the infant Pattie, abandoned by her mother; I felt abandoned and lonely in this constellation because Pattie either lay silently on the couch or talked adoringly about someone else, usually a new boyfriend.

Soon, splitting mechanisms were no longer evident in her remarks, even when under stress. In fact, fusion of self- and object representations was now her usual means of escaping anxiety. She was regressed below the level evident in her daily life and seen in treatment up to this time.

THE VERMIN STORY

Within a month of starting Step Three, Pattie reported a dream in which she was being pinched by a staple remover the sharp edge of which had pierced her skin as though she had been bitten by an insect. She had this dream after her parents had visited the farm with friends for a weekend and her mother had told her not to appear at the farmhouse but to stay in her own apartment. Although it humiliated her, Pattie did as her mother asked. She said it was her mother who had been pinching her in her dream, and who was "under her skin." She toyed with the word staple, noting that it was sometimes applied to food supplies. She needed her mother for nourishment, but her mother only gave her food with pain (the pinching). Staple also reminded her of the *stable*, which represented the rejection that forbade her the house and made her an animal in the stable.

After telling me this dream Pattie reported again going to bed with a stranger from whom she thought she had become infected with vermin in the pubic area. By her next session the vermin story had developed a life of its own, and she kept talking about almost nothing else during each session, as though she were reading one chapter after another from a book. By now she thought the vermin had infested every part of her body, and she was very fidgety on the couch. I thought the vermin had something to do with her dream about the staple remover. But as time passed I began to believe that there might be some truth in her story, although I decided not to intervene since she now seemed to be coming to her sessions just to tell me about the vermin, to ask what to do about them, and to have anxiety attacks. A week or so later she went on her own initiative to a dermatologist, who told her she had no vermin. This did not persuade her, but only made her consider the reputable dermatologist a nobody. Now she demanded that I check her body and once even lifted up her skirt, intending, I thought, for me to inspect her pubic hair. I told her not to do this, that I wanted to continue as her analyst but had no psychoanalytic technique to apply to the sight of her genitals. She never tried to lift her skirt again.

I explained that I had no idea whether she was in fact infested, or not, but that I had begun to think that her "vermin" were involved in her being about to tell me about something bothersome beneath her skin. I reminded her that only recently had she become organized enough to see for herself the meaning of the dream about the Nazi woman and to buy a new hat to fit her developing sense of self. I suggested that her preoccupation with harboring vermin might pertain to the process of finding herself, although I did not know how. I wanted to encourage her to go through her sessions in spite of her discomfort.

One day soon after this she declared after rising from the couch that she had left vermin on it, and the next day she kept itching as she lay there speechlessly. Sitting behind her in my chair, I felt regressed as though in a trance state when I suddenly realized that I, too, was itching all over. This awakened me to the fact that her "bugs" had evolved into a sort of transitional object in the sense that Greenacre describes (1970). She spoke of transitional objects being a bridge between me/mother and mother representations. The vermin created a meeting ground for our skins. By scratching at the same time, we were stimulating our skins and in a sense putting borders around ourselves (Elbirlik 1980), separating the skin of one from that of the other. We were trying to break our symbiosis by scratching.

I explained this to Pattie without using such technical terms as *symbiosis*, speaking instead of "psychological skins," the desire to be one with the other, to be separate from the other, and so forth. With this, she instantly surrendered her delusion about "bugs." Three months had passed since her first dramatic regression that had turned my couch into a pool of water. At this point we moved into the fourth step of her treatment.

Chapter 10

Step Four: The Second Split Transference

ATTEMPTS AT INDIVIDUATION

After our "skins" were separated, Pattie caught cold, coming to one session with Kleenex and cold medicine and declaring, "I think I'm dying." She reported a brief dream of the previous night in which she had dreamt of her birthday. I made the formulation that she perceived this as killing her fragmented personality in order to give birth to a new one.

The next night she dreamt of constantly passing gas, and then she dreamt of being in a warehouse with solid walls where she began rearranging furniture. She saw a desk of her mother's, which, in reality, was in the room of Pattie's older sister. In this dream she summoned up enough courage to ask the saleswoman, who wore a wig, if the furniture was hers. The woman, who seemed made of plastic (bad mother?), refused to give Pattie the desk because of "the nasty expression on her face." Upon this, Pattie loaded a gun but woke up at once, feeling anxious.

I explained that she was now working on an intrapsychic separation from the representation of her mother. I thought that passing gas represented her wish to exorcise her bad self- and object representations, and an expression of hostility in the hope of asserting herself. I also asked her to consider that by passing gas, by becoming offensive, she might be protecting herself from something. She said she was protecting herself from the mother who would not give her the desk.

What was important, however, was Pattie's curiosity about her dreams, and her trying to utilize them to gain more insight into her psychic functioning. After being unable to get the desk from her mother in the dream, she openly examined her jealousy of her siblings. She spoke of how her parents lacked empathy with her needs, and of how I did as well, something, she said, she had seen in me for a long time. Her parents were made of plastic, but I had acted just like a computer. Now, she saw that I was not just a machine: "You have empathy!" she declared.

A Budding New Self

That night she dreamt of being a beautiful woman enjoying the envy of other women. This dream expressed her wish to deny her needy aspect and to hold on to the split all-good and idealized aspect. She wanted a rebirth—if it would make her a glamorous woman. She had found a turtle on the farm; she thought it was in trouble and said she had saved it. I thought it represented a cocoon, a container of her budding new self. At this stage of her treatment she was still engaged in object relations conflicts, so when I spoke to her I noted the possibility that she wanted a new self, and protection within a shell. When the turtle died Pattie expressed much anxiety about dying herself and reported eating oranges to get an adequate intake of vitamin C.

Although she was no longer having one-night stands with strangers, she was having sexual relations with several young men, sometimes with those working on the farm, with whom she had at least some acquaintance. From time to time she would refer to one of these men as "a steady boyfriend." The staff member from the hospital where she had stayed occasionally visited her although, now married, he lived elsewhere. I refrained from advising her to drop him, but when she spoke of having to end this affair, I made approving sounds and commented that she seemed now to want to protect herself.

Pregnancy Reflecting Sibling Rivalry

One day she reported with bravado that she was pregnant. She spoke like a veteran and began making plans for an abortion. She had had to ask the putative father for money to have it. I did not get involved in the management of this crisis, but when we began work again after the abortion, I began exploring the meaning of what had happened. Different condensed elements were involved in her perception of aborting her fetus, but she connected it with her desire to rid herself of Mary, of whom the fetus had become a symbol. This time she did not place the blame entirely on the outside world but acknowledged some responsibility herself, even at times displaying a glimpse of appropriate feelings of remorse and the ability to look inwardly. Her dreams contained a body of water that I took to represent her and her mother's womb. There were dangerous leeches and cobras in this water, and she kept beating them over the head, at times seemingly aware that they represented her siblings. She exhibited no genuine mourning over the aborted fetus.

In one dream she and her elder sister pulled a trailer containing a horse. The trailer turned into a boat which she and her parents took to a family reunion, leaving the elder sister on the shore with the horse. Her mother turned to her and asked, "How about your sister? Should we go back and get her and the horse?" Pattie said, "No! She can take care of herself!"

She had this dream after seeing her sister's new baby. Their mother showered affection on it, while no one in the family knew that Pattie had undergone an abortion. This dream suggested that by becoming pregnant she had competed with her sister, and that she wanted to be alone with her mother—in her womb—and without her sister or her baby (the horse). She now understood that the horses represented, among other things, her siblings, and that she cared for them in order not to face her aggression toward them. But she sometimes beat them and was bitten and kicked in return. She did not yet show any remorse over the two horses she had shot when they had hurt their legs and which had become closely associated with Mary; nor was she remorseful over the flare-up of her aggression. (See A. Freud 1965, Volkan 1979b, and Schowalter 1983 on the uses and intrapsychic meanings of horses in the psychoanalytic literature.)

HEARING INTERPRETATIONS

Pattie still split her self- and object representations after her regressive experience in the third step and continued to be involved with issues of separation-individuation, although not in the same way as in the second step. Now she had a functional observing ego that could see with me the meaning of her behavior patterns. What was more important, she could see unfinished business from her childhood in her present activities. A childhood event she could now hear interpreted; her observing ego dealt with reactivation of her feelings toward Mary as a sick infant. Pattie mentioned that her "steady boyfriend" had complained one night of an upset stomach for which he wanted special food, including milk. The two went to a nearby store to buy it, and while there Pattie temporarily experienced herself as ugly and bad—the "big bad blob" self-representation had returned. After returning to her friend's apartment she felt she could not sleep with him that night. The idea made her very anxious, so she left him and went to a bar to find an all-good stranger. She found one, but now her observing ego told her she was repeating her old penis/breast-collecting pattern. She then saw the stranger as a bad man and left the bar. While driving to her apartment, she fantasied that she was my child, my *only* baby.

The dominant meaning of this incident is that the boyfriend, by becoming ill and wanting to be given milk, became for Pattie her sister Mary, who was physically handicapped as a young girl and who had robbed her of her mother's milk. Pattie envied her and wanted to murder her. Her sensing herself as bad and ugly was because she retained the derivatives of aggressive drive within herself. She could not sleep with her boyfriend for fear that she might murder him (her baby sister). She externalized her bad self-image onto the stranger in the bar, and later activated a good self-image and a good mother image in her fantasy of being my child. However, the idea that she was my *only* child represented her wish that the sick infant sibling had never been born. I interpreted this for Pattie. Patients like Pattie can make use of such interpretations in this phase of treatment.

FURTHER WORK ON SEPARATION-INDIVIDUATION

After three years of treatment with me Pattie said, "Now I know, I really know. It is true. My mother had a basic deficiency—she could not tolerate her children being loving and sharing toward one another. When my elder sister's husband goes away for a business trip, she comes home to my mother. No child ever really left home, psychologically speaking."

Her sessions became calm, and she made efforts to lead a more organized life. She bought folders to organize her papers and tried to keep her quarters clean. She finally gave up her apartment near my office and went permanently to the farm, driving the long distance to her sessions. She could not stay away from the horses. Although she spoke of unwashed dishes piling up, and the outrage of her parents when they came on weekend visits, I had not been able to learn whether she really kept the house like a pig pen.

She tried to become a horse trainer. Her father let her draw on her trust fund to buy a horse, which she stabled on the farm with her father's animals. Although it was hers, she was ambivalent about it, much as, she thought, her mother had been ambivalent about her in her childhood, but she gave it special care nonetheless.

In one of her dreams she was trying to escape from an orphanage to avoid being raped. I was beginning to understand more fully how separation-individuation struggles were frustrated when she felt rejected (raped) by the oedipal father. Her reality testing was still blurred, and splitting and projective and denial mechanisms still strong. She got nowhere with her effort to obtain a job. Pattie did take some positive steps forward, however: Her hours were no longer chaotic, and she was observing the therapeutic process with me and showing evidence of progressive moves.

A CRISIS IN THE ANALYST'S LIFE

At about this time I became preoccupied with the illness of my sister, who is six years my senior. Mental representations of external events can affect not only the patient's but also the analyst's participation in the therapeutic process. My sister, on a visit from her home in the Turkish Republic of Northern Cyprus, was to have undergone minor surgery when it was discovered that she had a brain tumor. Although it proved to be benign, its excision was risky and complicated, and many subsequent surgeries were necessary. She was in a coma for weeks; for about five months we did not know whether she would live or die, or, if she lived, whether she would have severe mental problems or be vegetative. As her brother and one of her two relatives in this country, I was deeply involved in her situation, which at one point seemed so hopeless that we talked of funeral arrangements. A memory from my teen years kept coming to mind. With my family I had gone to a Cypriot village where a play was being staged. We stayed in the home of a man involved in staging this play, which had a shooting scene. When I picked up a revolver I thought it was a prop for the play, and in fun I pointed it at my sister's head and pulled the trigger. Luckily, it did not fire, but to my horror I learned that it was a real weapon, and loaded. Now my own analysis of my dreams made me aware that I felt some guilt for the surgical invasion of my sister's head. My own psyche constructed a drama that resembled Pattie's intrapsychic story of guilt over wanting to have her siblings dead. Having had an experience so closely recalling hers, I found it hard to be neutral and distant enough to analyze her material.

During my sister's illness it was necessary to cancel a few of Pattie's sessions. I was outwardly undisturbed and was sure I could function as usual in my analytic role, so I decided not to burden Pattie with my personal preoccupations. She sensed my distress, however. My notes at that time make it clear that I was not aware of her reaction to my distress. I was not only denying my state, but was denying my patient's ability to understand me. Just as her mother probably did not know that young Pattie had been disturbed over her preoccupation with Mary, her ailing child, so I did not recognize Pattie's conscious and unconscious reactions to my acute grief over my sister. Once she brought a bunch of wild flowers, which she left on my table in an effort to save me from my distress, just as she had tried, at great cost, to save her mother. At the time I gave the flowers no thought but to regard them as a feminine gesture.

In retrospect I think that my getting her to verbalize her recognition of my distress, and my brief acknowledgment of it, supplemented with my supportive statement that I would keep on working with her, might have been helpful to us both. In any event, the important thing to do when something unusual happens to either the patient or the analyst in the course of treatment is to bring the event into the therapeutic process.

After a while I could not fail to see that Pattie was feeling that I had abandoned her. She had another dream about trying to escape from an orphanage, in which she did escape, was raped, and was returned to the institution. In the dream she looked like Shirley Temple as a child. Shirley Temple represented herself in search of new parents, seeking to be loved and as happy as the typical Shirley Temple character usually succeeded in being. Memories of the analyst she had had before coming to me, who had seemed to sleep through their sessions, returned. I was like her in failing to understand Pattie.

Pattie dreamt of being terrified at finding one of her stallions blind. There were no valuable associations to this dream, and it did not occur to me at the time that the blind horse might represent me. In another dream, a woman with bleached (plastic) hair, supposedly an expert fencer, was demonstrating but using the wrong maneuvers. Pattie wanted to correct her but asked herself,

"Should I care?" and then awakened. She went to the bathroom and then returned to her bed. A few hours later she awakened herself by wetting her bed and was shocked by what she had done. She wet the bed again the following night. I knew she was regressing again but now this regression was not in the service of reorganization and progress. I described her therapeutic regression in Step Three, from which she emerged with delusions about bugs and itching, a phenomenon we both observed, especially me. But the present regression was accompanied by extreme anxiety, and I was of little help. Recalling that her horses stood for various people and things, I feel now that in the transference I might well have been represented by the blind stallion who had been so good but who now could not see where he was going, or the expert fencer who was performing badly. But I failed to see such meanings at the time. Pattie's loss of bladder control reminded her of an attack of colitis she had had when she was 18. Her fear of a return of her colitis made me anxious as well, but I tried to conceal my anxiety.

Three weeks after Pattie lost bladder control for the second time, my sister had a crisis and I had to cancel a session with Pattie. At our next meeting she openly verbalized her recognition of my anxiety over my sister. This time I acknowledged that there was illness in my family and that I might be preoccupied with it. I went on to say that things had taken a turn for the better, which was true, and that I was fully able to work with her. I supplied no details and she asked for none.

RESCUE FANTASIES

Her next hour found Pattie well dressed and without anxiety. She looked like a young lady and spoke of being grateful to me. "I see you more and more as a person. You are not Volkan the computer any more." She spoke of feeling like an adult—"no longer helpless" and "what a relief to be grown up!" I was struck by her brave attempt to get well overnight. She seemed to be getting well and to be considerate, which in turn allowed me to relax a bit. The patient was becoming the analyst's therapist (Searles 1975).

She had probably behaved this way when she wanted to help her mother when the latter was disturbed over Mary's problem. I felt close to Pattie and appreciative of her efforts. I was mentally competing with her mother, who, I thought, had probably not understood her daughter's attempts to be helpful. I did not want to belittle her responding to my grief by making cold interpretations, so during this session I responded to her appreciation and her declaration of feeling well with the approving sound "Uh-huh, uh-huh." But at the next hour, to which she came again rather well dressed, she wanted to discuss *our* relationship. She recalled that she had been physically ill for a short time during the first year of our work, and that she had asked me to take care of her. I had agreed that it would be well for her to take care of her physical problems, but I had not looked after her nor had I recommended a specific physician. She said she now understood why. If I recommended someone, she would be depending on me. She said that because of me she had learned at last to take care of herself. "You forced me to teach myself how to take care of myself."

I responded that my recent preoccupation with personal matters might have played a part in forcing her to take care of herself, but that I was not sure how therapeutic I had been during the time and had been unaware that my preoccupation might be interfering with our work. I quickly mentioned my appreciation for her concern and her demonstrations that she was gaining control over her life. I suggested, however, that neither of us would want her apparent "wellness" to cover over any unresolved issues. I assured her again that my personal crisis was over, which was true since my sister had left the hospital and was slowly recovering at home. We resumed our work.

RETURNING TO THE FIXATION POINT

The very next day, Pattie dreamt the repeating dream of being a child and having gum stuck in her mouth. Her "wellness" had gone, and she had returned to her fixation point. In associating with this dream this time, I heard more details of her early life. Her mother had become pregnant when Pattie was teething. Pattie had kept a pacifier until she was 4, when her mother bribed her with a doll to give it up. She recalled nightmares in which she had been afraid of being gobbled up and afraid to eat. As a child she named the creatures that peopled her nightmares "mouth monsters." It was one of these that she had seen in the design on my couch before lying on it. She had "ripped out" her baby teeth before they were loose enough to fall out and had tortured herself by adopting the old trick of tying a string to the tooth and attaching the string to a doorknob and waiting for someone to close the door suddenly.

She could now understand, with my help, that the gum in her dream represented her being stuck in a kind of limbo. Symbiosis with the mother (swallowing the gum) and separation from her (spitting it out) were both perceived as dangerous, so she kept on chewing it.

A NONANALYTIC TRANSFERENCE

As we resumed work we seemed to have a symbolic beginning: My practice was moved to a new and more private office not far from my old one. I made the move for practical reasons, but I wonder now if the timing coincided with my motivation to fully commit myself to work again after my personal crisis.

Continuing on the road to health, Pattie said she wanted to try something she hadn't as a teenager. She thought that young girls usually became infatuated with entertainers, and she had seen a young male singer named Ken at a local nightclub. She often went to the club and fancied herself in love with him. I knew that her being "in love" was at least partly a resistance to therapy. She was finding a new love object because of her recent perception that I was rejecting her. Although I thought we had cleared the air about our relationship, she might still be unconsciously seeking a displaced transference love figure.

She seemed surprised when Ken noticed her. He was divorced, and they soon became lovers, with me a kind of spectator. I began to hear less and less that pertained directly to transference. My effort to explore with her the possible resistance aspect of her new relationship incited little response or curiosity. On the positive side, she was trying to have a relationship with only one man. Her parents disapproved of him, but when they were away he stayed with her.

When, at the oedipal age, she was disappointed with her mother she had turned to her father and had initially felt that he accepted her, but when he was depressed, he also disappointed her. I believed that if her turning from me as a representation of her mother to the singer, who represented her oedipal love object, was a repetition of her childhood experiences, her relationship with Ken would, in the long run, turn sour. Their relationship did last for a year, but then she withdrew from it, seeing Ken as a dreadful mistake, a person she had outgrown. During the time of her extreme infatuation with him I felt that her transference relationship to me was not active. It was as though she had left me (the mother representation) behind and had found a new love object. The oedipal father transference was being reenacted somewhere else. Although I usually refrain from interfering with such a development and wait for the process to take its course, I interpret the resistance involved in it and I know that eventually the father transference also has to come between patient and analyst and must properly be worked through in Step Five.

SECOND LOOK

As she embarked on her love affair with Ken, Pattie referred more often to important men in her life. At first she was curious not about her own father, but her mother's father. After moving some distance from the mother transference she was trying to understand what had led her mother to provide her with such deficient mothering.

I now heard, for the first time, that her mother's father was a rather eccentric millionaire living in seclusion in Dallas. In his mid-nineties, he was arthritic, confined to a wheelchair, and attended by a nurse.

Pattie was now curious about why her mother could not handle her children when they were all with her. Her mother had experienced strong sibling rivalry, her older sister being her father's favorite. The sister had been married and divorced three times "because no one could fill my grandfather's shoes." Pattie's mother was treated like a baby by her father and only had her mother. Pattie's grandmother died when Pattie was 12. She recalled that her mother changed then and "became like my grandmother," appearing more confident than before and wearing her grandmother's jewelry. But her grandfather could still make her mother lose her confidence and cause her to cry. Behind her socially acceptable manner remained certain hidden weaknesses; the facade was impressive but there was something wrong inside. Pattie began to realize that her mother's personality had an "as if" quality. Pattie began planning to go to Dallas to visit her grandfather, with her mother and brother. I realized that more than wanting to see her grandfather she wanted to observe the interaction between him and her mother. Canceling two sessions, she flew to Dallas, and on her return she was greatly excited over her observations.

This visit represented her attempt to have a *second look*. Using this term, Novey (1968) speculated as to why some patients in psychoanalysis or psychoanalytic psychotherapy have an urge to explore old diaries and other family papers and to return to the physical settings and the people who had been important to them earlier in life. Aware that in some cases such behavior may constitute acting out, he held that "in many more they constitute behaviors in the interest of furthering the collection of affectively charged data and thus helping the treatment process" (p. 87).

Pattie had observed in Dallas that her mother was still nervous in the presence of her father, now a feeble old man. Pattie felt that her mother's conflicts with her father had militated against her (Pattie) getting to know him. Now, to her delight, Pattie felt comfortable with the old man, and even with her brother, who had also been in Dallas. Although the old man was rather eccentric, Pattie saw his sophistication and pioneering spirit. He had a fine gun collection and had given guns to the children of his favorite daughter, Pattie's aunt. Pattie and her brother spent hours cleaning his guns at his request, and in return he gave each a gun. Pattie felt that this gift reestablished contact with her roots. She was angry at her mother for having failed to inculcate pride in her background.

It will be remembered that she had once wanted to be a man and had forbidden mention of penis envy lest it destroy her hope of having a penis. She carried herself like a male wrestler and shot horses with a gun her father had given her—a phallic symbol, she used it aggressively. Her reaction to the gun given to her by another important male figure, her grandfather, was different: She admired this valuable gun and as such she put it away (repressed it). Satisfied with the possession of a wished-for phallus, she could now move up on the developmental ladder and blossom as a girl. Soon after the Dallas trip she came to her sessions looking like an apache dancer in a red sweater, a beret, and a short skirt. Her attempted appearance as a woman on her grandfather's level of sophistication was a caricature. After giving a full account of her experiences while away, she declared that she would soon be 24 and felt "terribly ordinary." I said nothing to interfere with her effort to raise her self-esteem and to find "generational continuity" (Volkan 1981c) in herself.

In the first dream that she reported after her trip she had found herself in a house with a primitive kitchen and dirt floors like the house of an early settler. This no doubt represented her perception of her grandfather as a pioneer. "The kitchen was nice," she said, "even though it looked 200 years old." She concluded, however, that the kitchen housed unkempt people and contained no food.

In spite of her good experiences in Dallas, Pattie could not help recalling trouble in her grandfather's house. I later learned how ill he had been at the time of her visit, and that until she went to Dallas Pattie had perceived her grandfather as an eccentric who gave her nothing. "The trip was a test," she said. "I see things differently now." She collected all the pictures her mother had taken of her during the past three years and observed that in all of them she was pouting.

She then turned to her own father's background, seeking reasons for his depressive disposition. He had lost both his father and his best friend while in his early twenties.

Pattie was greatly excited over getting a letter from her

grandfather asking if she liked the gun he had given her. Although she was aware of the possible sexual symbolism of the gun, it was important that she be acknowledged by the head of the family and have a sense of belonging. She dreamt of traveling alone with her grandfather and becoming sophisticated under his tutelage. Associating with the dream, she spoke of its transference implication, that is, getting "sophistication" from me: "I look around and watch people older than I. They don't know a thing! But I am undergoing psychoanalysis. I am discovering what is inside myself."

Preoccupation with Death as Psychic Liberation

Then she suddenly became preoccupied with death. She was especially afraid that her horses would die. I told her that horses stand for many things. I suggested that her fear about losing the horses might reflect her attempt to liberate herself; perhaps she wanted the death of her old self so that she could reach a higher level of autonomy and independence. She must have understood what I said because her preoccupation with death disappeared.

RETURNING TO THE VERMIN STORY

Pattie, as we recall in Step Three, had had a dramatic therapeutic regression in which she had been preoccupied with a delusion about "bugs," which led to her intrapsychic separation from me as the symbolic mother in the transference. Now, attempting to individuate further, her bug delusion returned. She reported that her wrists itched. Her symptoms were not as dramatic as they had been in Step Three. She spontaneously recalled her previous preoccupation with bugs. She saw a dermatologist, who reassured her, and within a few days her delusion disappeared.

Childhood Fantasy of Pregnancy

In speaking of her new preoccupation with bugs, she recalled having had acne as a teenager and speculated that she might be "visiting" her unresolved teenage problems. When she was 12, a boy had taken her behind some bushes and tried to engage in sex. "I was able to say no then," she said and recalled how upset she had been over the episode and how dirty it had made her feel, especially in her skin. This brought to mind a childhood fantasy that she could be made pregnant by skin contact. This time, then, following her preoccupation with death, her preoccupation with "bugs" and itching, although still in the service of separation-individuation and the establishment of body boundaries, included another condensed but higher meaning—one pertaining to childhood sexual fantasies and defenses against them.

With bravado she invited Ken to the family farm when her parents were there. She wanted to prove that she was not dirty! Although her parents knew that she and Ken were lovers, they chose to ignore the fact, although they lectured Pattie on the importance of a young woman's reputation. A compromise was arrived at: Ken stayed in the house but the couple had separate rooms.

At her next session she declared that "adulthood means that you have one lover, no more casual sex." She had recently seen at some gathering one of the men with whom she had had casual sex and who had stolen money from her. She now said she could not remember his name.

When she was 12 she had gone to a fair and then to a party with other youngsters, and did not leave for home on time because she was enjoying herself. She had put on lipstick for the occasion. Her father had driven to the house where the party was taking place, insisting that she leave with him and humiliating her before her friends. Noticing her lipstick, he called her "a slut." Weeping, Pattie asked him to apologize, which he did reluctantly, without understanding how deeply he had hurt her. "I've never cried since then," she said.

RESOLUTION OF NONANALYTIC TRANSFERENCE

I found that another meaning of Pattie's appearance as an apache dancer was to test me to see if I would respond as her father had.

I passed her test in the most silent but effective way—by adhering to the therapeutic position.

We had been working together for three years and three months, and her sessions and her reports now seemed better organized. She was reporting more events from her childhood and teen years, but there was no "hot" transference story. I was still providing a holding environment and being treated in general as the mother who was left behind. Her relationship to Ken was "hot." Although aspects of the father transference involving me appeared from time to time, they had not evolved into a full-blown transference neurosis. I made the formulation that her separation-individuation was not fully complete as yet; she occasionally gave evidence of splitting her self and objects, which, before long was reflected in her relating to me and Ken. When Ken was "good," she made no reference to me, but when he was "bad" she would make me "good." However, on the surface most of her activity seemed in general to be "extratransferential."

I refrain from seducing patients like Pattie into speaking of transference-related issues. If such seduction occurs, the transference issues usually tend to become resistances, and their interpretation and resolution may prove to be false. One must maintain the classical analytic position and wait for the natural evolution of the transference neurosis.

The Analyst's Response to Persons in the Patient's Association

When Pattie said, "What I am learning here is growing up," I tended to agree. I offered no gratification of her wishes but explored them with interpretations, clarifications, and, sometimes, with suggestions. I actively kept the working alliance and mutual curiosity alive, taking care not to side with people who appeared in her stories. I very seldom used their names in talking to her, however much she offered them. My interpretations and clarifications dealt with my formulation concerning *her* perceptions, expectations, and unconscious wishes. In a sense I focused not on the characters of the drama but on the author's motives for "creating" them.

Oral Greed

She kept speaking of her Dallas visit two months after her return, telling how her grandfather's regard for her had boosted her self-esteem. She reported that Ken now wore a beret, and that she had dreamt he was speaking with a "pseudo-French accent." Even *he* seemed to join her in her new "sophistication." She now began seeing him as totally "bad" and began referring to him as a freeloader, as indeed he seemed in reality to be. My formulation of her present view of him showed him as a greedy "mouth" always raiding the refrigerator. It seemed Pattie's bad oral greedy self was deposited on him. She wanted to be rid of him, but, as in projective identification, she had an empathic connection with him as the bad object. Although she spent hour after hour with me deploring his evil nature, she resumed her life with him when she left my office, only to return later for another 50 minutes of criticism of him. Then, suddenly, he would be "all good," as though she had forgotten describing him on the previous day as nothing but "a greedy, dirty mouth." Then she would talk of leaving the farm and the horses and beginning a new life in California with Ken.

I discussed with her the similarities between her current relationship with Ken and the relationship she had had with her mother in the earlier years of her treatment. Splitting her mother's image had led her to have a split image of her boyfriend. I explained my observation of her attempts to move away from her mother's orbit and to have successful relationships with men. She was cautious because of a fear of rejection by men (her father) and was still bringing into her relationship with men a model of her relationship with her mother. I explained without using technical terms how she had been a satellite (Volkan and Corney 1968) of her mother when she first embarked on her treatment with me, and how in recent months her sessions had been filled with an account of how she was orbiting around Ken. I told her that I had for some time seen her as the moth and her mother, and later Ken, as the flame. She listened intently and told me she understood that in spite of all the progress she had made symptomatically, she was once more settling into limbo. She wanted us to move on in our therapeutic work.

That night she dreamt of being in a car parked on a slope. She put the car in reverse and pulled the parking brakes. The car began sliding backward. Afraid of hitting someone, she awakened with anxiety. I connected her dream with my remarks about her satellite state, and suggested that she wanted to regress therapeutically in order to move away from limbo and to a higher plateau in her treatment. Something, however, probably the fear of aggression (hitting or killing someone), was inhibiting her. She responded by saying that she certainly would perceive a moth's meeting the flame as dangerous.

To "Kill" in Order to Individuate

After this session, Pattie left for a family celebration of Christmas. Returning in early January, she reported having felt left alone, rejected, and humiliated by her siblings. She observed again how unable her mother was to tame the siblings' rivalry and to protect her from the sadism of the others, especially the elder sister.

She then allowed herself to reexperience the thoughts and feelings of her early teens. With considerable affect she described in detail her attack on her mother with a serrated knife. "Hitting someone" in her dream was connected with her unconscious notion that her mother had to die if she were to become a completely separate individual. After the tense session in which she recalled the attack on her mother, she failed to keep her next appointment. When she did come, she admitted to being flooded with murderous fantasies, which were now directed toward me as well; she had skipped her previous appointment for fear of killing me. "I can't go backwards!" she screamed. I told her that the moth was examining the flame, and that if she could tolerate it, so could I.

Over the next few days she reported being ill and was overcome by laziness and sleepiness. I told her that her supposed illness was her way of protecting herself from realizing her need to "kill" her mother in order to individuate, and that there are different ways of "killing." The truth was that we were speaking of psychological (symbolic) killing rather than murder, even if she had intense and alarming emotions associated with it. If she chose not to go through this, she would stay in a state of limbo (satellite state). I told her: "I am not telling you to get well. I am telling you that if you want, you *can* get well. When you say you *can't* go backward, or you can't go forward, I hear you meaning that you *won't* regress or progress because you want to protect yourself from alarming feelings."

That night she dreamt of being with several girls who had been her classmates in elementary school. Their identities were confused and all were having oral sex with one another (lesbianism as a kind of symbiosis). They also grew penises they could suck. Then the dreamer smelled something burning and saw a fire. She woke up screaming. I thought that the moth had met the flame!

Drastic Changes

During the next few months she made some drastic changes in her life. She took a position at a horse farm, nominally to break in young horses, but actually to clean out the stables. She complained about this work, but finished out her contract, which took about a month. In the manner of a business proposal, she spoke to her father about building a stable on the family farm, and he consented to her plan. She bought another horse with her own money.

She had her ears pierced—a symbolic gesture toward becoming feminine—and became preoccupied with repairing old furniture, working to make her quarters as charming as possible. I still could not determine whether her room in the farmhouse—and the farmhouse itself—were simply cluttered, or really sordidly dirty.

She finally moved to rid herself of Ken, who had been unemployed for a long time and continued to be "a greedy mouth." She dreamt of becoming a man and murdering him, holding the idea that she could not then be identified because of the sex change. Then she thought of her pierced ears and decided that her plan was not practical.

The same night she dreamt that her mare, which was in foal,

had been hit by a car and had suffered a broken leg, so someone shot it. She awakened, screaming, "You have no right to kill her! Her leg could have been fixed!"

RECAPTURING CHILDHOOD DEPRESSION

We discussed once more Pattie's desire for separation–individuation, and her perception that she had to kill the representation of her mother and the corresponding representation of herself as "the greedy mouth" in order to achieve this. In her dream, the killing of the mare represented a combination of killing her pregnant mother and her sister Mary, who had leg problems. She again visited the psychogenetic aspect of her conflicts, which were precursors of her guilty feelings. This time her "murderer" self was displaced onto an unknown person, gratifying her superego. She finally confessed to feeling remorse for shooting the two horses earlier. It came out that one of them had been in foal.

Pattie seemed overwhelmed with childhood memories during her next sessions. "My rescuing some and simultaneously wishing to kill others is a very old syndrome, isn't it?" she asked. I agreed, and she *began to cry*. I was moved by this and remained silent in order to let her experience sadness at this level without interference from me. She was recapturing the childhood depressive affects that she had been unable to tolerate. She spoke of her constant pain as a child and her longing to be adopted to escape it. "Why do I feel all this again now?" she asked. "To master it!" I replied. Although this was true enough, I felt my remark to be inadequate in view of her emotional flooding (Volkan 1976).

She spoke of feeling her old emotions "as if I am starting all over," adding that, at the age of 7 or 8 when she realized that her father would be of no help to her in dealing with her problems with her mother, she had undergone a personality change. "Everything reminds me of when I was little," she explained. "I was so depressed, paranoid, and frightened!" Then her sadness gave way to laughter: "I am feeling my old feelings, but at the same time I can't stop laughing. It is good laughter. I spent years in therapy, years in the hospital, lived with the animals, killed animals, but I think I am slowly breaking the cycle." I felt that she was referring to the orbit of the satellite state.

Her interest in repairing furniture increased, and I told her this activity represented an attempt to repair herself. Within a month she asked Ken to move out. "I did this by myself without calling anyone to justify this or that," she said proudly. I said nothing, and during the hour I learned (1) that she had received what she called "a business letter" from her father before asking Ken to leave and had been pleased by the thought that she and her father might after all become "business partners," and (2) that she was spontaneously ready to talk about *us* as the patient and her analyst.

She was now showing a direct interest in her father, still hoping for him to redeem her childhood disappointment in him. She was excited by the possibility of becoming his business partner. At the same time, she was declaring her unwillingness to express thoughts and feelings about me more vividly. With Ken, an extraanalytic transference figure, removed, I thought she might be ready to develop a transference neurosis, and that we could proceed to Step Five. Pattie was approaching her fourth year in treatment, three years and eight months into her analysis.

Chapter 11

Step Five: The Development of Transference Neurosis

PEACOCK STORIES

No drastic event marked Pattie's move from the fourth to the fifth step. For many months she vacillated between these steps before she could be considered neurotic and no longer on a lower level of personality organization.

What follows is my understanding of her transition as evidenced in her "peacock stories." Her last attempt at therapeutic regression in Step Three had occurred when she dreamt of driving her car backward and had been anxious over this regression lest she hurt someone. With my encouragement she recaptured the memories and feelings of her murderous attack on her mother. Now her ego allowed her to tolerate a detailed recollection of this event. This therapeutic *regressive* move resulted in her individuating more effectively from her mother's representation. She gave up Ken, who stood for aspects of Mother, Father, and her "greedy mouth," and she was now ready to become involved in a *progressive* move, which symbolically became evident in her speaking about peacocks. On the farm, she was raising baby peacocks in a caged area, and when they matured enough she released them from the pen. The act of freeing them made her anxious, representing her breaking away from the satellite state. She feared their being eaten by foxes and racoons once they were given their freedom, but to her delight they survived and flew about. She knew they represented her sense of self.

The night that she freed the peacocks one of her initial symptoms returned—she slept in the barn. However, in discussing this we understood that this symptom was now used for a different psychic purpose than when she had been afraid of human contact and sought safety among the animals. Now she was sleeping in the barn with the newly liberated peacocks to assure their safety for the night. In the morning they would be freed again. Pattie was making herself into a good, nurturing mother, one who would protect her children but also let them move out of her orbit at an appropriate time. This behavior symbolically made up for what she had not received from her own mother when she was a child (Volkan 1982a, 1982c). Once the good mother was created and Pattie had absorbed her functions, Pattie had a chance to advance through regular developmental channels.

Symbolic Meanings of Peacocks

We discussed her unconscious choice of peacocks to symbolize aspects of her childhood problems and her triumph over them. The cry of a peacock is like that of an infant, and we equated pea*cock* with a penis. Thus the birds represented Pattie's helplessness and the power to deal with it. The possession of a penis was in the service of her differentiating from her mother, and soon Pattie realized that she was no longer obsessed with having a penis, although she was still ambivalent about this obsession. She knew that further progress in her treatment would lead to her surrendering this obsession. Her main symbol for her fantasied penis was still the prized gun given her by her maternal grandfather, to whom she had written without receiving a reply. Her initial excitement about getting to know the old man was gone.

She would not give up the penis (gun) easily. If her grandfather was feeble, she could cause her gun to be "recathected" in the transference. Thus an aspect of the transference neurosis dealing with sophisticated psychosexual issues and structural conflict was evolved and sustained for some time, signaling full entry into Step Five.

Having heard of a *physician* (representing her analyst) who gave skeet lessons, she enrolled, taking her grandfather's gift to her lessons. The gun would thus not be used for aggression—the killing of horses, or the murder of Mary or their mother—but for a "tamed" sport, and thus she could still keep her "tamed" penis and have it approved by the physician (analyst).

During one skeet lesson the physician received a summons to care for a man with a badly cut arm. He exclaimed, "Shit!" and went on shooting for another half hour before taking his emergency call. When he did leave he failed to say goodbye to Pattie and seemed to ignore her altogether. The next day she came to my office with a tight mouth and an unhappy expression. When I asked the cause of it she reported having dreamt that her grandfather had given her a bent rake—for cleaning "shit"—instead of the gun. The dream's day residue clearly came from the events at the shooting lesson. She had desired pride in her roots and so had gone to the physician to improve her ability to use the gun her grandfather had given her. But the physician's exclamation "Shit!" had symbolically given her ordure. He was not compassionate and failed to give adequate care to his patient, with whom Pattie identified. The prized gun had turned into a bent rake.

The physican's attitude reminded Pattie of her childhood. Her mother was not compassionate, and her father failed to approve of Pattie. "I have my childhood feelings," she said, and angrily demanded that I interpret the dream at once.

I told her that she perceived me as one who would not understand how much her prized gun meant to her. She was not really ready to hear my interpretation and would probably nullify anything I tried to say.

Wish for Premature Termination

She was angry toward me for a month, declaring that she was all right now, and that we could terminate treatment. I told her that although she had freed herself from her mother as she had freed her peacocks, she still wanted to be free and have a cock or a prized gun, and that she was perceiving me as someone telling her to be free without a penis. She had come to the point in her analysis at which she was thinking about becoming a woman but also considering that this could only be achieved by the surrender of something she had formerly highly valued. Her progressive moves in the past had made her anxious; now they added to her anxiety by making her face a conflict between wanting to keep and to give up something of value.

These remarks were the day residue of a dream she reported on the following day. In it, she was driving a car that went forward this time, representative of her progressive move. When she came to an intersection (the point in her analysis I had spoken of in her previous session), she wanted to stop but could not because the brakes would not hold. When she tried the hand brake (a penis), it failed too, and she was terrified at the likelihood of being run over by a huge truck. There was no collision, but her terror awakened her. The dream suggested that speedy progress was risky, and that without a properly functioning penis she might be crushed by the huge truck, which she called "a real prick!"

I told her that I was in no hurry, but observed her desire for a speedy recovery. Could we not stay for awhile at the "intersection" and see what kind of choices she might make? My calm remarks about her nightmarish event had a soothing effect, and her hostility toward me vanished. However, she could progress only by returning to one of her symptoms. She began coming anywhere from 5 to 15 or 20 minutes late to each session.

Being Late to Sessions

Formerly, when afraid of her aggressive impulse to kill me, she would skip a session and sleep all day. Her new habit of being late, as I understood it over time, was her security control—a control over her working through her separation–individuation problems. She would use her 5, 10, or 15 minutes of tardiness to separate herself from me as the preoedipal mother. With the establishment of this habitual control, then, she could move on to deal with me as the oedipal father or the representation of people or things of higher-level investment. I interpreted her habit again and again over a period of time, and she understood and agreed with me. In spite of this, she kept being tardy for most of the rest of our time together. In view of the severity of her preoedipal problems I thought that her coming late to her sessions was a token of triumph that she could not give up. To be sure, she had worked feverishly to resolve object-relations conflicts in order to move upward to confront structural conflicts, but in a sense she could control with her tardiness for sessions whatever object-relations conflict might remain, and thus move on to deal with the structural ones.

The Analyst's Peacock Fantasy

After grieving in various ways over the surrender of her penis, she would ask me to guarantee her success as a woman. The meaning of her preoccupation with peacocks changed. Now she was interested in a hen peacock and the hatching of eggs and the emergence of chicks.

My family had recently acquired a new house that stands in a woodland, and as I listened to Pattie's account of her peacocks I thought I would like to have some too. I envisioned them strutting across my grass and perching in the trees outside the living-room windows. I wanted to ask Pattie to give me a pair of the baby birds, but I would never ask for such a gift nor abandon my technical stance. I was so involved in my patient's therapeutic story about the birds, and I enjoyed hearing about them so much, that I had my own peacock fantasy. I knew that when Pattie became a woman and gave up her penis she would want to create a substitute by having my babies, and a baby peacock stood for such wished-for babies. My fantasies showed how much we were attuned in this process of making a woman out of Pattie!

She stopped making any mention of her mother during her

sessions, and I amused myself by imagining that her mother was assigned treatment during the initial five minutes of her sessions she chose to miss herself.

A MAGICAL TOY

One day, cleaning her room, Pattie found the magical toy baby bottle that she had stolen and with which she had fed rats. She brought it to a session and recalled again, with intense affect, the story about her mother that caused her to steal the bottle. She asked me if she could keep it on my desk, wanting to keep it between us so its meaning could be analyzed. She indicated that she still had a conflict about keeping it or disposing of it. I agreed that she could leave it on my desk with the understanding that we would analyze its psychological meaning and then she could take it and dispose of it. The bottle stayed in full view on my desk. I told her it was another controlling device keeping her from slipping back into her mother's orbit, as was her habit of coming late to her sessions. Under these conditions she could examine her relationship with her father and with men in general. She eventually took the bottle back and threw it away without ceremony. Its magic was gone, but she kept using her other safety valve—her tardiness.

THE FATHER OF TODAY

After we had analyzed Pattie's story of the baby peacocks, she made an effort to be friendly with her father, who responded positively at first. He occasionally came to the farm alone and took Pattie out to dine. Although she continued coming to my office in dirty jeans, she said that for the candlelight dinners with her father she dressed in an appropriately feminine way. Soon, however, Pattie became disappointed in him. He sounded to me like a depressive character, and there was no pleasing him. Although their encounters, in which Pattie had had so much hope, turned into shouting matches, she stuck with him and tried to influence him. He accepted her as a business partner only on his terms, and it was clear he saw his daughter as a sick girl. Masochistically, she undertook more and more responsibility for the work on the farm, which now had a flock of sheep and some new horses. Her father never gave spontaneous expression of approval or appreciation of her efforts, and when she demanded acknowledgment it seemed insincere to her, although he occasionally paid her a few compliments. After watching this cycle of her solicitation of tenderness from her father for some time, I spoke of it to her, and we both expected it to continue while her reaction to his shortcomings became gradually less painful.

After Ken left and she began trying to recapture and modify her oedipal life, Pattie was virtually abstinent sexually. Once highly promiscuous, she no longer needed sexual activity for the resolution of preoedipal issues. She could not, in fact, indulge in sex since the oedipal issues were not worked through. On the infrequent occasions when she did take a sex partner she felt satisfied biologically, being able as she had not been with her pickups in the past to reach orgasm. She felt the need, however, for psychological satisfaction and announced that she wanted to find someone with whom to fall in love. She was nevertheless aware of having many intrapsychic issues to deal with first.

I told her that it was unlikely that unfinished issues concerning her father, influenced by her childhood experience, would be resolved by trying to recapture and change her relationship with her *father of today*. I said that her daily preoccupation with him was a resistance to bringing such unfinished business from her childhood into the open for us to confront.

MANIFESTATIONS OF EROTIC TRANSFERENCE

Since sharing the peacock stories, Pattie was even resisting viewing me as a man. She was controlling me by separating us for five minutes or so as though I were her mother, and she was trying to resolve her problems with men outside her sessions. Although she understood my interpretation of her resistance, she stayed cautious about returning to a charged oedipal transference neurosis.

When she had felt rejected by her father when he had become depressed over the loss of the recognition he had counted on, she was 8 years old, and the rejection robbed her of the hope of having an integrated self and high self-esteem. I offered her her last chance to alter things for the better, and if she failed to accept, there was no hope for her. She seemed sensible about it, and I encouraged her to take this chance when she felt ready. Instead of agreeing to go back to oedipal issues in her sessions, she gained weight and began to look most unattractive. Her overeating had many meanings, including her desire for motherly love, but its main purpose was to make her sexually unattractive. "You are building up a wall of fat between us because you don't want to be disappointed in my possible manly love for you," I said.

She began to diet and tried to make me sexless. She recalled how terrified she had been when I first told her that we would work together with her lying on the couch. "At the time, I sexualized this, but I didn't tell you about that," she said. "It terrified me, but I took the chance. But, you see, you never screwed me, so I trust you."

I told her that I was pleased to hear that my behavior had made her trust me, but that I now heard a different meaning in her statement—that my not making sexual overtures had not made her feel anxious because it indicated the absence of a functional penis. I asked if she could imagine trusting a man who still possessed a functional penis. I also reminded her that she had recently referred to me again as a computer and thus made me sexless. Although she could allow herself to have sexual thoughts about me, an oedipal father transference that could be systematically worked through would not develop. She would say, "It is useless for me to have these feelings anyway; we will never go to bed together. Also, you are too old for me!"

I noted that the possibility of having sexual feelings for me was too much for her to handle. She began bringing one of her dogs with her, leaving it in her car in front of my building while she had her session. She brought another dog that she even taught to run loose around the building during her sessions. I thought she saw the dogs as chaperones. She would not cooperate in exploring the meaning of this behavior.

ATTEMPTS TO RESOLVE INTRAPSYCHIC CONFLICTS IN CONCRETE FASHION

Pattie was becoming more skillful as a horse trainer and thought of the possibility of studying veterinary medicine. This pleased me, and I told myself that my pleasure reflected the importance placed on education and the attainment of a professional degree in my family. I realized, however, that she was not ready to tolerate a rigorous school schedule and that it was doubtful that she would qualify for college. She did not go to school, but undertook on her own a program of reading and began making reference to social and political issues. I came to consider her highly intelligent.

Her fifth year of treatment found her still living at the farm, although she often had spoken of moving out. In reality she could not afford to move. Her talents lay in the horse business, and she was unable to support herself independently. She worked hard at improving relations with her father, and after some struggle they made a deal to buy horses from Europe, keeping them on the farm for training and subsequent sale. Pattie made an effort to improve her acquaintance among people in the business of selling and breeding horses, which she realized offered lucrative financial possibilities. With financial support from her father, a training ring was set up on the farm, and a skilled European trainer was brought over to train the animals and to give instruction to Pattie. The employment of this man, Klaus, necessitated a trip abroad on which Pattie accompanied her father. After a two-week sojourn with him, Pattie seemed to have gained confidence, but she began to perceive Klaus as an unwanted sibling and to complain that her father was so stubborn that she disliked traveling with him. She did not tell me of a dramatic event that had taken place on their trip since she was not conscious of its meaning. It was disclosed in Step Six, but had I known of it upon her return I would have better understood the meaning of her dreams at the time. On the manifest level, her dreams dealt with some sexual occurrence that took place while she slept. She also dreamt of being crucified or trampled by horses, as though for being guilty of something.

She filled her sessions with her hatred of Klaus. I did not challenge her interpretation of this excessive dislike as reactivation of her old sibling rivalry. Had I known of the events in Europe I might have noted how her preoccupation with the familiar, old sibling rivalry issue was used to resist the conscious acknowledgment of another unresolved issue. Klaus stayed in the house with Pattie, and I learned that sharing the house with him in the absence of her parents caused her to feel sexual tension that she needed to deny.

I have observed in my practice that patients like Pattie who have been severely traumatized in childhood have a need to use their "parents of today" to reexperience their childhood. As though talking about and understanding their childhood is not enough, they have to resolve things *concretely*. Pattie had done this with her mother and was attempting it with her father. I knew that she was capable of forming a lasting transference neurosis about oedipal issues, as she had done with her peacock stories at the start of Step Five. Now, a year after hearing these stories, I still awaited her development of a "hot" oedipal transference to me.

Although she had had high hopes of the European trip she took with her father, she was still disappointed in him, and began telling me that there was no possibility of being friends with him. She planned to retain their business relationship and continue living on the farm, but thought of finding new relationships with other people.

Recalling Childhood in Actions

At five years and three months into her analysis she arranged for a significant activity involving both parents. This time she was most cooperative in her free associations, so *both* of us understood the intrapsychic aspect of what she had done. After seeing an advertisement for a special seminar at a rather distant university, she enrolled herself and her parents, leaving Klaus to look after the farm. The seminar dealt with equine anatomy and diseases, with special reference to reproduction and the delivery of deformed colts. During the few days of the seminar, Pattie shared a motel room with her parents, sleeping in the bed with her mother while her father, then in his early sixties, slept in the second bed. Thus Pattie was their *only* child! Moreover, a slide show of foals with deformed legs provided a representation of Mary. Pattie talked to her mother about Mary's childhood, and she was now less defensive over hearing Pattie's claim that her troubles had begun with Mary's being deformed at birth. Pattie's memories of Mary as a child poured out, and she recaptured specific memories of her mother's being unkind. For the first time she experienced a primitive form of powerful guilt. While sharing a room with her parents Pattie was flooded with memories of her childhood "mouth monsters" and witches. She had one dream of a mouth, representing her oral greed, being smashed. She exchanged roles with her mother, creating good mothering for the little Pattie in an effort to undo the mother's original ineptitude as a parent. She saw that her father was unaware of what was going on. On the return trip he had the car radio turned on but not set to any station, and he seemed content to listen to static. Pattie thought this symbolized the way in which her father put a buffer between himself and other people. Her hope of changing her parents and reconstructing her childhood with them disappeared. Although I knew she would still struggle with her hopes, by now she had done sufficient reality testing to know that her neurosis would not be resolved in this way.

Searching for Objects for Identification

After they returned to the farm one of their horses went berserk and she beat it. I was never sure whether or not she had purposely aroused it, but she hit its mouth, which probably represented her oral sadism. I felt that the animal also stood for her parents and Mary. Although she knew that beating it was not as bad as killing it, she was very remorseful, asking a knowledgeable woman horse trainer what she could have done beside beating it. While she was talking to this woman on the telephone, her father kept calling her downstairs every few minutes asking her to wash the dishes. She was furious at his interference, but was able to listen to the woman's advice, which consisted of a recommendation to use a tranquilizer. The woman added, "The most important thing is that you protect yourself when a horse goes berserk, so you don't get hurt."

Pattie found a similarity between me and this woman, saying, "The most important thing is that I am coming here to see you to find out different ways of handling my emotions and my life." She adamantly declared that she would leave the farm, and although I said little I knew that she could not yet manage this. Then she burst into a long, cleansing sob, displaying real grief over losing the hope of changing her parents.

THE VERMIN STORY AGAIN

Pattie felt more energetic and better integrated in the following sessions and exhibited two phenomena. First, she brought a white flower in a pot to a session, which she had bought on the way to my office not for me but for *herself*. I felt it represented the birth of a new ego, one of which she herself could take care. She spoke of forming a better and more civilized relationship with her older sister. Although the siblings lived in different states, Pattie had become friendly with Mary, who was also in treatment. At times they compared their understanding of their past. Although they could never become close friends, Pattie had considerably improved her relationship with her other brother and sister. Klaus had by then gone home, but Pattie spoke of her growing prowess as a rider and trainer of horses.

The second phenomenon occurred in the very next session. She returned to her tale of being infested with vermin. Now, however, she had no delusions, saying that the first time she had spoken of being infested there was every likelihood of this being so. She had met a woman of her age who was having sex with a very ugly man. Apparently, Pattie had identified with her and then wished that her new friend would be different from others who had disappointed her. This woman looked like an animal, having flea bites all over her arms and lice in her eyelashes. Pattie had thought of cutting the woman's hair, but felt that cutting it would brand her. This led her to associate with the branding of Hester Prynne in *The Scarlet Letter*. Discussion of this allowed her to see that she was feeling guilt for her oedipal sexual wishes. The story about vermin contained elements from the oedipal level.

She reported dreaming of being in a European hotel with a girlfriend. The room's doors did not close, so her friend went freely from room to room and slept with different men. Pattie did not want to do this; she wanted to be able to say "No." I would have understood the meaning of this dream more clearly had I known what took place on Pattie's European trip. Her associations related to her development of more stable boundaries by being able to say "No" to her impulses and to other people. She recalled how, during her original experience of "having bugs," we had both itched and developed psychological borders between self- and object representations.

She said she felt herself to be in a transitional state. Although she commented that she had dreamed of a European country, the country might have been Persia. She was reading about Alexander the Great and Persia and thinking about me at the same time. This was the start of her sustained return to an oedipal transference neurosis with me. She kept trying to identify my native land and finally recalled, on the basis of what someone had said, that I was from Cyprus, "near Persia." We were both Alexander the Great, conquering new territories in her psyche. She then directly associated me with Alexander. When her readings disclosed that Alexander had been a homosexual, she decided that I was not in fact sexless, but a homosexual who was no threat to her. She could continue to deny her sexual feelings for me.

It was at this time that the hospital worker who had gotten her pregnant called her, and it gave her great joy to say "No" to his suggestion that they get together.

OEDIPAL TRANSFERENCE

In order to change an appointment, Pattie called my home. Later she spoke of her fantasy of having spoken to my wife there, whom she perceived as a young woman. She asked me if she were in her twenties, saying that if this were so, I frightened her. I finished her sentence—"since sex between us (a young woman and an older man) would then be a real possibility." When, at last, she declared her love for me, she blushed furiously. She was very shy and alternated between denying what she had said and affirming it. During this time she lost six pounds and looked very pretty.

She had not had sexual relations with anyone for seven months, nor could she recall masturbating during that time. When she was 27, five years and three months into treatment, she arranged a date with a man totally different from her truckdriver pickups. When she had intercourse with this gentle and rather effeminate man, it was of very brief duration, but she had wanted to give herself, to keep things under control, to be a sexual woman. A few weeks later she had intercourse with someone she had known for a long time and enjoyed it greatly. She thanked him for satisfying her, but realized that he was too self-centered to appreciate what she was going through. Considering him callous, she never slept with him again. Often in her transference she said that she was in search of a man like myself to love and with whom to have children.

Practicing Motherhood

She became friendly with the mother of two small children with whom she spent a good deal of time. "You know, I am practicing motherhood," she said, "and I like it." Recalling her two abortions, she declared, "You know, I could have two children myself." Although she experienced remorse and grief, she knew that if she had delivered her babies she could not have been a good mother to them. "Besides, I want my children's father to be a man as mature as you," she said.

She was changing rapidly. Her lumpy fat was gone, and she bought new clothes, including a black dress "to mourn my old self." She also bought a watch, feeling that keeping track of time is an adult activity. She had a series of dreams she called her "high school dreams." They concerned her years in school, when things were very bad for her; she said the dreams represented her desire to go back and start over on a different track. I heard from her the typical girlish Cinderella fantasy of finding a rich man and marrying him. She brought a picture of her bedroom for me to see; it showed a nice, tidy room in which the bed was neatly covered with a lace-bordered bedspread. I had the answer to the question I had asked myself in the past as to whether or not she lived in squalor. She may have done so at one time, but no longer. She was obviously inviting me to visit her bedroom—as a father aware of her sexuality, or at least as a father who would accept her femininity.

When I asked for her associations, she said that when she was 15 her whole family went to Europe, renting a three-bedroom chateau for the summer holiday. She was "a big bad blob" then, and no one wanted to share a room with her, their rejection being very painful and humiliating for her. She was now showing me that she had an enviable room of her own. She associated further, saying that her father did not allow her to close the door of her bedroom at the farm, and that she was determined to shut the door for privacy, to have a feminine room and the privilege of inviting whomever she chose to enter. In the next session, remarks about her having a bedroom in a house she did not own led her to consider real-world issues, and we continued doing this during the months to come.

FURTHER TAMING OF AGGRESSION

By now the farm had 22 horses, 66 cows, 60 sheep, six dogs, five cats, and one peacock, and although a farm manager was employed, Pattie carried an unbelievable workload caring for the animals. She loved the farm, saying "It is the most beautiful place on earth." But since her parents were aging and Pattie had no title to the place, she was singularly unprotected; on the death of her parents her siblings would be sure to sell the place. I encouraged her to get legal advice about her future, since although she was not paid much for her work, it was offset by her free lodging, and she had started to pay for her treatment from her own funds.

The result of this discussion was that she persuaded her father that she needed more help with the farm. In the sixth year of her treatment she came to a session highly excited, announcing that now she would be a "boss" and wanted to assimilate all the administrative skills I exercised as medical director of the hospital in which we held our sessions.

At the start of the sixth year of treatment, there occurred an event that had significant symbolic meaning: A yearling broke its foot and instead of destroying it, Pattie nursed it back to health. She recalled the earlier shootings and declared that her aggression was now tamed and that "a horse is a horse; a horse is not Mary!"

A Killer Image within the Patient

Her next session signaled a major intrapsychic change in Pattie. She had brought with her a blood sample from a horse, putting it in the refrigerator near the waiting room, planning to take it to a veterinarian when she left my office. She asked if she had been right to do this. I approved, but suggested that we pursue the possible meaning of her behavior. It turned out that she had wanted to demonstrate to me that drawing blood from an animal was not killing it but benefiting it, and that her aggression was tamed. She recalled awakening the night before and recalling a dream in which she was in the house of her childhood with a pathetic looking man who was a killer. She then dreamt of deciding to get rid of him by poisoning him.

She knew that the killer was herself—her aggression. "I killed the killer in a womanly way—by poison," she said. "He had no remorse, but I had feelings for him. But he had to die!" She was able to make her own interpretation, and went on to show that in the past she had turned her aggression on herself. "I was abusing my body with drugs and alcohol. Once I thought my body would die. The dream certainly is about my taming my aggression. I now think that I will live a long life. Children give people a purpose to live. I'd like to have children."

Recalling her shooting horses, she commented that she was in a risky business, that horses could kill her, but that her increasing professionalism as a trainer made her career less dangerous. The dream reminded her of her childhood home. She remembered that her mother had collected many things from her father, but would not use them; the ornaments only gathered dust, the mother treating them, according to Pattie, as she had treated her children. Most of them were now cracked, faded, and in some way flawed.

She had visited her friend with the two children, one of whom fell down and hurt himself while she was there. When his mother soothed him Pattie wondered what her mother would have done under the same circumstances. She remembered breaking some rice bowls as a child, and wondered if she had really wanted to "break" her mother.

WISHING TO HAVE CHILDREN

Pattie spoke again of having children of her own and treating them quite differently from the way in which she had been treated. "A weird thing," she laughed. "I'd like to have your children, but I can't imagine having sex with you." While watching her friend's little son sleeping one day she saw his erection. She was fascinated at seeing how a boy's body functioned. To her, the erection stood for a kind of freedom that the boy had. She now thought of her horses as representing freedom. She could relate to the small boy and the horses differently, with pleasure but without envy.

The character of her hours with me was changing, but she continued to speak of wanting a child. For the first time she mentioned terminating treatment. "I want to have a baby to replace you when we stop working together," she insisted, adding, "It is so amazing what we have done here!"

She reported feeling "solid." I could detect a symbolic reference to her identifying with me. Severely regressed patients like Pattie at first identify with the analyst according to the step of treatment they are in at the time (Volkan 1982a, Tähkä 1979, 1984). I earlier noted Pattie's identification with my integrating functions, and she was now identifying with my functions as an analyst and as a catalyst for change in her. She spoke of an old horse with "old habits," saying that I "would not allow her to continue her old habits. With patience, and without losing my temper, and not being 'kind' all the time, I helped the horse to change, and she responded well."

At the same time, she was telling me about her effort to rid herself of her disruptive identification with her parents. She noted that she did not need to be as rigid as her father, nor scatter-brained like her mother.

THE HIPPOPOTAMUS

In examining one of her dreams, Pattie directly freed her old oral aggression without anxiety or symptom formation. There was a hippopotamus with huge teeth in this dream. It bit someone on the leg, representing Pattie causing Mary's leg problems out of anger. She reported having had the old chewing gum dream again, "But it was not intense. Before, when I had this dream I would wake up with sore jaws. I must have chewed furiously in my sleep. But now I did not experience this intensity."

The hippopotamus in her dream also represented her obesity, although she was no longer overweight. She recalled our discussion of how her fat tissue was to keep herself sexually undesirable to me. She had recently seen a television account of sexual harassment of female patients by male therapists, and said, "I have full trust in you. In fact, I'm looking for someone like you, but younger."

TAKING STOCK

Pattie began beautiful recitals of all that analysis had done for her, and how she now perceived important people in her life with whom she had formerly felt conflicted. For example, she could now say of her mother, where formerly she would have reported a painful exchange, "My mother is a good-hearted person, but, you know, she is a lost cause."

When she asked when we would end our work I suggested that we take stock of where we were and decide on a mutually agreeable time. In the next session we began taking stock.

Real-World Issues

In two-and-a-half years she could have real control over her money, but she questioned now whether her father should control her trust fund. They had begun selling horses, and, having other money, too, she was paying directly for her treatment. She felt secure in money matters, and had not consulted a lawyer about her legal rights as I had suggested because she believed that would have been tactless. She could keep her options open.

Her Relationship with Her Parents

They were now perceived in more realistic terms than before. She felt close to her mother and had a business relationship with her father. She still felt their influence on her, but no longer buckled under it, being now able to test reality.

Her Relationship with Her Siblings

Her older sister was no longer an archenemy. Although she thought of him as narcissistic, Pattie liked her brother, whom she seldom saw. She now felt comfortable with Mary, to whom she wrote and whom she called on the telephone. She felt no obligation to join the family at Christmas.

Male–Female Relationships

After long periods of abstinence she had intercourse a few times, always reaching orgasm. She was now selective in picking sexual partners. She had no steady boyfriend, but wanted to have one like me. She did not want to put off terminating her treatment until she found one. She would take a chance on terminating first. She still felt some doubts about her femininity and thought she needed more work on it, but she liked her friend who had children and had become interested in motherliness.

Her Love for Herself

She was much less masochistic. She could invest libido in herself without thinking of herself as a femme fatale. She did not depend on a good mother's availability to have self-esteem. She wanted to lose more weight.

Her Relationship to Animals

She was aware now of how she used horses as symbols of many people and things. Her new ability to manage and care for horses enhanced her self-esteem.

Her Aggression and Impulsivity

All expressions of pathological aggression were gone, and she now used it to assert herself. She had better control over her impulses.

Self-Observation

This was greatly improved.

Responsibility

Pattie was responsible for her work on the farm, but her frustration with her father still interfered. She was coming to her sessions on time more often.

After taking stock, we agreed to work for six more months. At the time of this decision she had been in treatment for six years and one month.

Chapter 12

Step Six: The Third Split Transference and Termination

What follows is an account of Pattie's clinical progress during the six months before termination. I give events sequentially as she reported them. The reader will note her initial constructive response to the setting of a termination date; her review dreams; her anxiety, which led her to "visit" her old symptoms; and her new efforts to restore herself once more on a higher level. Her return to splitting was not as dramatic as I have seen in others with similar psychopathology (see Jane's termination phase in Volkan 1976, Chapter VI). However, she gave a strong illustration of returning to a magical linking object when she used a pillow to control the separation. Both oedipal and preoedipal elements "stuffed" in the pillow were analyzed and interpreted, and this led to her recapturing and tolerating—for one last time—her original pathogenic infantile fantasy. The resolution of such a fantasy validates her work with me as being psychoanalytic. References to her mourning appeared and reappeared during this time.

REACTIONS TO THE TERMINATION DATE

When Pattie asked for a termination date I did some soul-searching, being aware of my old habit of coming to the rescue of women in trouble, a result of my having been born in a house of mourning and perceived as a replacement child for an idealized dead uncle (see Chapter 3.) One of my "missions" as a small boy was to rid my mother and grandmother of their grief. I dealt with the conflicts arising from my background by sublimating (Volkan 1985c), but the tendency to try to save women in distress surfaced from time to time. I recalled how pleased I would have been had Pattie been more idealized and better prepared for veterinary school. I recently found myself agreeing with her that she would look better if she lost more weight. When I caught myself doing this, I told her that in the past, hidden under her "big bad blob" representation, she had entertained the notion of being perfect, and now I was in a way wanting her to be more perfect by losing weight. I was making a technical mistake by speaking so, and I took some responsibility for this, but I added that we should consider the possibility that she was passing to me, as termination approached, her own old desire for perfection, so that I had become the agent to push her toward this end. I warned that we should both be alert to this.

I had to consider whether, regarding the termination date, my desire to "save" her completely might obstruct my agreeing to let her go. It was then that we agreed to conclude her treatment in six months. Two days later Pattie reported having worked very hard on the previous day to clean her house. She had installed storm windows "to keep the heat in," and had begun to wash the outside of all the windows. She knew that her energetic housework had something to do with our decision to part in six months. To her, "Keeping the heat in" meant "keeping my impulses under control," and the window-washing reflected her efforts to look prettier. "The place is sound and OK," she explained, "but I must clean up a few more dirty windows."

Outer Change versus Inner Change

During the next few sessions she reported progress with her window-washing, and soon it was all done. "The outer change does not necessarily show the inner change, but it will not hurt me to learn more about how to look as a young woman." She was going to a spa, taking exercises. There she met a beautiful woman who wore a bikini but disclosed none of her pubic hair. Eager to learn more feminine secrets, Pattie questioned her about how she managed this, and was told that the woman shaved to accommodate the outlines of the bikini.

Within days after setting a date for termination Pattie wore her hair differently, purchased new clothes, wore conservative lipstick to her sessions, and rejoiced in being able to tame a stallion in less than five minutes. She then sought out a young man for a date and stopped smoking. She became the very picture of a healthy young woman. I refrained from comment since I did not want her to stay that way—dependent on the support of compliments from me; she should now stand on her own feet. When she appeared half an hour late for one session, she spent it going over memories of rejection by her depressed father. I said she might have perceived me as the depressed father. Was she expecting me to say something that would acknowledge what a healthy woman she had become? When she replied that she had, we discussed the possibility that she could maintain a high self-esteem without depending on applause from others.

In her next sessions she wandered through extreme views of herself and then tried to take stock of her present state as a woman. When she sold one of the horses imported from Europe she could indeed call herself a businesswoman. The sale brought excitement along with sadness and gave her a chance to review her mental representation of horses and their meaning to her. "But basically," she said, "I treated the horses like I treated my parents. I was attached to them but yearned to be independent of them. I felt sad about parting from the horse I sold; I felt as if my own child were leaving me. But I think I was now separating my horses from their symbolic meanings and coming to be a businesswoman."

A Review Dream

In the third week after deciding to terminate, Pattie reported a long dream that I felt summarized her analytic work. It began in her childhood home, but she was searching for a new home and observed that the neighborhood had changed. She sensed her mother's influence but could not recall seeing her. She found four bins full of water and covered with stone covers. She went into one of the bins, which was like the inside of a cave, with a mysterious and exotic quality, possibly like something from the Near East. It was warm and she felt comfortable.

She said the four bins stood for her parents' four children in their mother's womb. She visited "being in the womb" in her analysis by entering the womb of an analyst from the Middle East (I am from Cyprus). She dreamt of adventures in the cave, including disposing of a snake that she kept in a bottle, invisible to anyone but herself. She finally went through a tunnel, in a rebirth fantasy, to get out of the cave and find a nice home. (I noted that the idealization of analysis might be a resistance to her mourning over losing it.)

The next day a dog on the farm killed a sheep and had to be destroyed. She felt sad about this although the dog had been a troublemaker. Before having the dog put down she had considered other options, and even thought of advertising for a new master in spite of the fact that she knew it would not make a good pet. That night she dreamt of being in a house into which newcomers had moved, bringing with them a new breed of dogs without feet that were cruel to people to revenge the cutting off of their feet; they were messengers of evil.

Pattie knew that killing her dog had activated her childhood rage toward Mary, represented by the dogs without feet. It was as though her own rage had caused Mary's problems. Although she wanted Mary disposed of, she felt guilty. I thought that this time she was reviewing early conflicts that had affected her all of her life. It was a moving hour. She spoke of raising orchids, and I sensed in her a tenderness the quality of which had escaped me before. She spoke of how until now nursing her untamed rage made her feel that she was not entitled to the good things in life. She returned to her "review dream" about going into a bin, recalling now that the bins were located on the property of the family of a boy who went to school with Pattie and whom Pattie secretly admired. When he once asked to hold her hand he was offering her what she so strongly desired, but she seized his hand and flung him to the ground, hurting him. After this he stayed away from her. Pattie spoke tearfully now of how she had "defended" herself from things she greatly desired but did not feel entitled to, and how she thus had held tenaciously to her "big bad blob" image, hiding her tenderness and longing for tenderness from others.

MOURNING AND INTERNAL AND EXTERNAL CHANGES

The sessions that followed were full of mourning. "I think how I was, and I feel sad," she declared. "I am mourning over things that were part of me. I know this is a transitional state, but God it's painful!" She had made an effort to give up smoking and added, "I think giving up smoking relates symbolically to my losing bad parts of myself. I never knew how to mourn properly. I always had guilt and depression with my mourning, but now I know that there can be mourning without depression and guilt."

A month and a half after setting the termination date, and after her open mourning, she was busy creating a new self. "I have no excuse for being sick any more," she said. "This is a peculiar feeling." She enrolled in a new health spa and lost a few pounds very quickly. She looked very well.

While making these external changes she spoke openly of internal changes taking place—her identification and her desired identification with me. "The only other person I know who is like you is me," she said. "I don't really want to be an analyst, but when I talk to other people I need to weed things out. I am too analytical. I am at a different level. This really freaks me out."

She was strongly attracted to a young man named Steve, who came to work on the farm. Since he remained on the farm at night sometimes, she contemplated having an affair with him in order to have the missing element before finishing her analysis—having a steady boyfriend. Instead of acting on her impulse, however, she wanted to know Steve first. "I began listening to him like you listen to me," she said. "This is a wish approach; sex doesn't run my life any more."

THE APPEARANCE OF AN OLD SYMPTOM

While infatuated with Steve, Pattie suddenly felt "dissociated" and went to a bar where she picked up a stranger with whom to have intercourse. The next day she was greatly worried about being infested with vermin, and when she came to her senses she told me with great embarrassment what had happened. I said nothing at first except to encourage her to continue analyzing. Still embarrassed, she spoke of having felt very well recently, and wondered why she had gone to the bar and repeated her old symptoms. She said the man she had picked up was not "a scum*bug*," but an attractive man. Although she had been "dissociated" during the whole experience, she kept thinking that she would have to tell me about it, and that she would feel very uncomfortable. Then she began shouting, "Fuck you! You're a failure!"

It was not clear whether she was addressing me or uttering what she expected I was thinking of her. "I suffer, but I get you, too! I don't go down alone!" she declared.

She recalled that after work with her psychologist she had felt better, but had suddenly felt depressed again. Her parents had rushed her to her therapist, who became very alarmed, saying, "I was afraid something like this would happen." When, soon after this, Pattie was admitted to the hospital, she felt betrayed.

"I am repeating what I did with her and what I did millions of times with my parents," she said, expressing appreciation for my not being dismayed by the return of her symptoms. Instead of telling her that I was afraid she could not be cured I said, "Let us continue to analyze."

The fact was that when she told me of her picking up a stranger I did *not* feel like the little boy she flipped over when he offered his hand; I could still keep my hand out to her. I believe that such tolerance, which is not easily acquired, comes from long experience with patients like Pattie. After telling about her lapse I said that an analysand may have in termination phase a tendency to visit old symptoms as though to say goodbye to them. I was glad that she had not revisited her old symptom just for the sake of repeating the past, but had done so in an effort to understand its meaning. She began her next session by saying that she did not like revisiting her old symptom. "I don't need to repeat it, I can analyze it," she said, adding that her recent infatuation with Steve, her experiencing of sexual feelings, and her visit to the bar were all "manifestations of *transference*." I cannot recall ever having used this term with her, and I was delightedly amused that she had not only correctly identified the source of her behavior, but was using the correct term, which she had picked up somewhere. Any question as to where she had picked it up would be an interference with her serious search for its meaning. She spoke of leaving me and of psychologically leaving "the old family nest." No wonder she wanted to know if the old breast/penis could still be found in case of difficulty in her progress.

REVIEWING PARENTAL INTROJECTS

Pattie's parents were visiting the farm, and she watched them very carefully. She was amazed to see how much she had internalized their bad parts. She was discovering that what she had taken to be her own self had been to a high degree composed of parental introjects. Searles (1978) warns against interpreting such findings early, since it would be injurious to attack the patient's core self, which consisted of such introjects. Moreover, premature interpretation is injurious "if the analyst gives the interpretation in a spirit of disavowing implicitly that he himself possesses, in his own personality-functioning, any appreciable element of the particular personality-traits in question, for an interpretation so given tends to foster the patient's feeling isolated from (1) his usual sense of identity, (2) his parent from whom the introject had been largely derived, and (3) the analyst" (pp. 19–20). However, in the termination phase these issues are mutually examined.

Pattie noted her mother's behavior, which she summarized as a secret declaration that "I can't do anything—I'm not smart enough." She watched her father telling himself that he should be harsh at all times. Reporting these observations, she said that I never used her weakness against her, and that she never experienced me as being harsh with her, although I left her with her own harshness, which was the end result of, among other things, her introjecting her harsh father. When she wanted to get rid of her own internal harshness by putting it on me, it did not fit, and she found this maddening. Her going to the bar also was partly an effort to make me harsh. Putting her internal harshness into me would comfort her. The option of disowning the harshness without externalizing it onto me never occurred to her.

WISH FOR NEW IDENTITY

Pattie dreamt of being visited by a representative of a school who sought to enroll her as a student. Pattie was dressed conservatively, and the room where the visit took place was full of geraniums. In reality Pattie had, at the age of 20, been enrolled in this school, which emphasized its riding program, but she did not ride well and could not handle her life there. She greatly disliked one female teacher and left within a few months. However, the school kept sending her its alumni news bulletin, and every year she cynically and mockingly sent it a donation of one dollar. The day residue of her dream came from her having received the bulletin that day.

The dream represented her desire to live this part of her life again, this time with a different identity, one which would not alienate those whose world she wanted to enter. She had taken a geranium plant from the school, potted it and cared for it so well that she still had it after many years. The geraniums in the dream were her secret link to all she wanted to be—an unaggressive and socially acceptable woman who need not separate from the school.

She amused herself by cutting up and then trying to tape together pictures of herself; it was as though she were trying to make a new Pattie. "Sometimes I feel like a jerk wearing sweat pants and going to a health spa. But no matter what, I will go through with it," she said. Noting that she was about to turn 28, she asked, "What is my marketability?" She expressed sadness over her lost years. I too felt sad and told her that we had no choice but to be philosophical about those years.

She reported becoming rather a sensitive rider and keeping the horses' stalls clean. "But," she said, "I envy myself in my recent dream—conservatively dressed and comfortable with my femininity. I'm not there yet." She reported writing to a friend what she had learned in her analysis, and how inner and outer needs had changed and how her inner and outer worlds now seem compatible.

FIRST REFERENCE TO A MAGICAL PILLOW

Three months after setting the termination date Pattie began talking about a pillow she was making. It seems that before she had gone to the hospital where she had stayed so many years earlier, she had bought a pair of pillow cases to embroider, which were stamped with a design of warriors on horseback. She resumed work on them now and thought of giving me one for Christmas, which was approaching. She said that completing the pillow paralleled the completion of her treatment. She now thought of the battle scene she was embroidering as a scene from the Middle East, one that represented her analysis. She enjoyed her sewing and put forth her best effort. She said she was happy at the thought of making me a present—it was not a bribe since she wanted nothing in return. Thus, she said, there was no need for me to analyze her gift and spoil her pleasure in giving me something. I said nothing, and before long she went with her father and Steve to Europe to buy horses. She returned just before Christmas.

The trip had been a business success and she had daydreamed about the handsome men she saw on the planes. "I am in a state of metamorphosis," she said. "I am not yet a flying butterfly, but I am certainly no longer a caterpillar!" She reported that my pillow was finished except for being taken to a shop to be stuffed.

She decided not to join her family for Christmas, but was surprised to find herself feeling some sentiment about them. She gave her own Christmas party, and that night dreamt about a famous male ballet star who was then being seen in a film. She talked to me as a young woman talking about a fantasied lover. When she went on a long automobile trip with Steve, who did the driving and had the car radio turned up high, she put plugs in her ears and daydreamed about Steve, *in her mind* undressing and making love to him. "I had fun. It was very enjoyable," she said. "And at the same time I was not involved in inappropriate *actions*. To have thoughts, desires, and feelings without immediately acting on them is a new kind of freedom for me," she added.

SHARING A BED WITH FATHER

At the start of the new year Pattie dreamt about a famous equestrian widely admired by horsemen. She was eating ice cream in the dream when this man asked to lick it. She felt highly flattered, but he took away her ice cream and walked away from her. The manifest content of this dream was that someone she saw as sexually important to her wanted her ice cream, which probably represented her breast, and then humiliated her. This dream signalled her telling me what had happened during her first trip abroad to buy horses.

Her disclosure was made after her father came to the farm for a visit at the first of the year, to be followed a day later by her mother. He was angry at finding cats living in the house, and while driving to her session Pattie thought she would end up talking about the same old issue—her anger toward him. She did not want to waste time doing this, but found herself muttering, "*Fucking* father!" She said that being alone with him was really bad, but when her mother was present she provided a buffer between father and daughter. Angrily, she added, "I was happy about one thing on the last visit to Europe. I didn't have to share a room with my father!" The significance of this remark escaped her. When I encouraged her to tell more, she disclosed that during the first trip for buying horses they had occupied the same room and that for some reason they had moved the twin beds side by side before retiring for the night.

As she told this, the significance of it struck her and she felt "weird." She recalled having argued with her father before they went to bed. "Oh my God!" she cried, "If we didn't fight we would fuck! That would be worse!" She called her relationships with her father "an aggressive love story." After calming down, she again reviewed her difficult early relationship with her mother, and how she had hoped to be loved and appreciated as a girl by her father in order to escape her mother, and blossom. He disappointed her and had smothered her hope of having high self-esteem as a girl. She now understood that she had been relating in a negative way to him in the hope of gaining his attention, using him to *confirm* her negative identity. At the bottom of all this, however, was that she really still wanted his affection and repeated an oedipal scene in order to see concretely what this was all about. She had not finished her associations to this incident when the hour came to a close.

At the next session she was beautifully dressed and wore perfume. Her mother had driven her to my office and was waiting outside for her. I asked if her mother were providing a buffer between us, noting that if this were the case we might find it hard to talk more about the bedroom in Europe.

Pattie said that Mary had made a one-day visit to the farm with her mother, and that this had given Pattie a chance to observe the attachment between them. At the table, their mother acted as though there were not enough food for two daughters. This did not depress Pattie, who was able to see it as a repeating phenomenon, in which she would then turn to her father. Suddenly she said, "My father screws Mary *too*!" She wanted on one level to express disappointment in her father, but on another to indicate that she had an aggressive love affair with him.

At her next session she showed me a new coat and gave me a warm, sensual smile. But as soon as she lay on the couch she started speaking of being fed up with her father. She complained of the condition of the ring they had built for exercising and training their horses, saying that her father showed no interest in *her ring* and that he was *"screwing"* her. When she realized what she had said she gave a nervous laugh, but I felt she was really ready now to face unresolved oedipal desires without much anxiety and the formation of symptoms. "I don't really want to sleep with my father," she said, "above and beyond the moral thing. I don't like him as a man; but I am amazed to see how much I was stuck with him when I was a child." She said she now understood that staying on at the farm was "being screwed by him." She had recently visited a friend who was a mistress of a married man. I asked if she also felt like a kept woman on the farm. "What a tradeoff!" she exclaimed. "In order to seek gratification for my childhood wishes I had to stay neurotic, a kept woman."

FREEDOM FROM NEUROSIS

Pattie spent the next few sessions telling me of her relief at having discussed her "secret." I don't feel helpless any more," she said. "If I stay on the farm, that will be my decision. It will be because I like horses!" She made a realistic assessment of her financial situation. Careful not to encourage her to make a drastic change, I helped her assimilate things, telling her that as time went on she could make her own decisions about the future and decide where she would live. "I feel alone now," she said. "I gave up my father in order not to be alone in the future. Anger still comes out, but I turn it into assertion."

In what she called a "wonderful dream," she had been skiing on a mountain. "I put the skis on. I was part of them. They were not foreign to me. Everything flowing, no chasing, no confrontation. I am having the best time! Me and my mountain! I am in control." Her associations recalled an unhappy experience skiing with her family, when she had felt humiliated by her inability to ski well. She had been left behind. "I really want to ski," she said. "Of course, I can't ski as I did in the dream, but at least I know that I conquered my childhood fear—the fear of abandonment."

In her next session she gave an example of how she could now change anger into assertion. When she had been transporting some horses in a horse trailer, her helpers had been careless and not listened to her directions. This made her angry, but instead of shouting at them she calmly called them together and told them how to do their work. Her handling of them had been successful.

On the previous day she had been in a checkout line at the store, well dressed and feeling confident. She ruminated over how her childhood conflicts had made her stay with her parents, and how they in turn unconsciously encouraged her masochism. The horses had dominated her life, and before that there were mice and hamsters. "Who the hell wanted to spend time with rodents?" she asked herself. Now she was doing an unbelievable amount of work on the farm and wanted a respite.

Lost in these thoughts, a man in the checkout line asked if she were angry. Surprised and jolted by his inquiry, she replied, "Thank you for your concern. I'm not angry any longer, just tired—just plain drained." When telling me this she began to sob. From time to time she stopped long enough to say that her sobbing made her feel more free. Then she reported a newly unrepressed memory. She was a child, feeling sick. Mary was crying and her mother was taking care of her. Pattie began to cry, too. "My father made me stop," she said. "He grabbed me and threw me across the room. I stopped crying." She kept on sobbing and spoke of her stubborn determination to change her parents. She really wanted to create good parents in order to be able to trust again, but she met with obstacles in carrying out this "project." When the time came to leave, she looked at me with tears in her eyes, saying, "I can cry freely now. Progress, huh? Thanks." I think she sensed that I was deeply moved.

Effective Grief

She told me later that she kept on crying all day. Little more than two months of her treatment remained. Recalling that her father had thrown her across the room, I asked whether she expected that I would throw her out. She replied that although she did not anticipate that, she sometimes felt as though I were telling her to "piss or get off the pot." She said that fixing a termination date had motivated her "to do things that I knew inside out." But she confessed to being sometimes frightened at the idea of not seeing me again. She said I was a god in her mind when we started work. Later I had become a machine, a nonhuman object, and then I was a doctor charging her for listening to her. Now she thought I was the most important person she had met in the twenty-seventh year of her life.

She was sad when I cancelled a session in order to attend a meeting. "Again, I feel like crying," she said. "It is as though I were losing my best friend." She was now able to tolerate grief readily. Before their treatment, patients like Pattie are unable to grieve effectively (Searles 1982). She now said, "What makes our separation tolerable is that I am not needy anymore—but sometimes the real world sucks!" She went on to give an example of what she meant and indirectly disclosed her identification with my ability to deal with day-to-day problems.

She met a young woman who was friendly to her and joined her for lunch, greatly pleased over this extension of her social contacts. At lunch the woman disclosed that she was a lesbian and admitted to sexual interest in Pattie, who calmly replied that she had no homosexual inclinations. She was, however, able to get the woman to discuss her very traumatic childhood. Pattie responded empathically, and when the two parted, the other woman felt better.

SECRETS IN THE MAGICAL PILLOW

Two months before termination, Pattie reported an important dream about the woman in the Nazi uniform who had appeared in a dream in Step Two. Although in this dream the woman seemed to be a sophisticated and elegant lady, Pattie recognized her. She gave Pattie a basket of foreign language dictionaries (German, French, Russian, and perhaps even Turkish). Pattie thought this was a great gift and had no fear of the donor. She knew that she represented me. This time I was a different kind of mother, still somewhat distant and controlling, but a helper. I was associated with Sigmund Freud since some of the dictionaries were in German. His work had been translated into many languages, and I had given her the language of psychoanalysis to communicate with her unconscious. Her associations led to "my pillow" that she was going to give me. In the dream I gave her a gift in return. The day residue of the dream was her asking her mother to take the pillow to a shop for finishing. She said it was not ready at Christmas because she still had ambivalent feelings for me at that time. Now she was ready to give it to me. She spoke of the paintings in my office, which were from different countries, one being Mexican. She could not have any associations with it. She supposed that some others were the work of a patient or patients who had left them with me to remember them by. She, too, was creating something to give me. It was like baring her soul.

She picked up with this when starting her next hour. Speaking of the pillow, she said, "You have to accept it. I have to give it to you." "I don't want you to forget me," she continued. "I don't think you will throw it away. You can take it home, but I think you will keep it in your office as you keep the paintings."

I thanked her for wanting to give me a gift, and said I appreciated the work that went into it; from what she had told me, the design was very complicated, requiring careful work. But I asked why she would think I needed a pillow to remember her by. If this were the case, the pillow contained magic, and if we were to leave a magical object unanalyzed between us it could be an agency of regression. I suggested that she might have some "last secret" locked up in it.

The Terrible Turk

She then recalled that I had once referred to myself as "the terrible Turk." I vaguely remember this. It was in the first year of her treatment, when she was filled with paranoid anxiety about me. I had tolerated her externalizations and projections and tried to be playful so she would not perceive them as dangerous when they returned to haunt her. She said that for a year after this she had mentally called me "TTT"—The Terrible Turk. She made up rhymes about this while driving to her sessions, such as "TTT is tea and pee." She was being playful with the terrible Turk image and her externalizations and projections in order to tame them through identification with my playful self. Nonetheless, a potential for real danger lay under this playfulness.

She said that the design on my pillow looked like a battle between crusaders and turbaned Turks. I suggested that one last secret locked in the pillow might be her negative feelings for me. If she gave me a symbolic representation of a battle between us, she would not need to speak of aggression between us.

I recalled her "aggressive love affair" with her father. Although she had said she was now free of him, I wondered if we needed to understand our relationship in terms of its reflecting that with her father. Since she had a pair of pillows, one of which I could rest my head on while she rested hers on the other—we would be sharing twin pillows as she and her father had shared twin beds.

She confirmed my thoughts, saying that she had taken my pillow with her on her last trip to Europe with her father and Steve. She was amazed to realize the meaning of this odd behavior: On her first European trip to buy horses she had "gone to bed" with her father, and on the second, she wanted to go to bed with my pillow—symbolically, with me. However, to defend against incest in the transference, once she was at the airport in Europe she lost the one piece of baggage that had the pillow in it. (It was later found and sent on to her.)

At her next session, she had a most friendly smile and greeted me with a friendly "Hi!" "Let's go back to the pillow story," she said. "I have thought more about it, and about what you said yesterday about my taking it to Europe. What is not finished in our work is contained in the pillow. I agree with you." So we went on to analyze her "last secrets."

She recalled having seen a mouth in the design on my couch when she first started work with me. She had been afraid of sliding down into it when she lay on the couch. She had been preoccupied with her mother's image and its reflection in me for some time—until the first dream of the SS woman. Sometimes she thought of me as a man and thought that lying on the couch had sexual connotations. Later, after the first dream of the SS woman, she would imagine my coming up to her as she lay on it, but she never thought of my really attacking her. She had entertained ideas like this as her treatment continued, but until now had never spoken of them to me. She had in fact thought for several years of giving me the pillow, but had not spoken of it then.

She had fantasized recently that I would reach out and touch her while she lay on the couch. It would be "a good touch," she said, and imagined my hugging her to show that I thought her to be a desirable woman. After she had this fantasy, she went to a party and flirted with a young man who was attractive and danced with her. His date confronted them with the accusation that he wanted to take Pattie to bed. Pattie thought this out of line, and he said to his date that he would not do such a thing. When she insisted that he had planned to bed Pattie, Pattie told her that he might indeed have had such an idea, but that "it takes two to tango," using a phrase she had picked up from me, and that she would not sleep with anyone she did not know well. Leaving the couple, she felt very proud at feeling no guilt, asserting herself, and acting calm and scrupulous.

Preoedipal Secrets

Pattie thought the pillow was like the bottle she had kept for years—a token of triumph over her separation anxiety. For Pattie, my keeping the pillow would preserve her forever in my eyes: Her oedipal secrets, concealed in the pillow, were analyzed, and she was now bringing her preoedipal secret into consciousness. At one level, if I accepted and kept the pillow, the dependent child Pattie would stay "alive" in me since I would be the one to be stuck with the pillow as she had originally been stuck with her stolen bottle.

I decided to tell her about the paintings in the office, which I had moved to after my sister's illness. They had not been part of the decor of my original office. Since we were close to termination, I did not want them to remain a mystery to her, and I also wanted her to see me as a real object uncontaminated with transference blurring.

I told her one was Mexican. She said that she had imagined her peacocks in the painting, substituting peacocks for the doves in the picture. Another painting, which had not been given me by a patient, depicted a butterfly over a forest. We now understood one aspect of her using butterfly symbolism to refer to gaining freedom from her archaic introjects. I told her that all the other paintings had been done by one of my nieces, but that it did not surprise me that she had concluded they were the work of a disturbed patient, because in some the faces seemed fearful and anxious. I reminded her of a time when she had sensed my anxiety (see Step Four), and I had reassured her that I had enough control of my faculties to continue working with her. I explained that my sister had been gravely ill when her daughter had made the paintings in question, and because she, too, was deeply worried, they no doubt reflected her troubled state of mind. Calling her attention to some very soothing colors and sensual figures in another of her paintings, I said that the artist had been capable of expressing other emotions as well.

I asked if she would be surprised if I told her I was not in the habit of accepting gifts from my patients, not because I failed to appreciate them, but because I thought the analysis of the wish to give a gift was more important. She said she was not surprised, but before the hour ended she insisted that I accept her gift. She wanted to leave an open door leading back to her neurosis.

REVIEWING OLD IMAGES

The next day she wanted reassurance that my caring for her was genuine. She wanted me to be her loving father without incest. She recalled again the hotel room in Europe where she had shared beds with her father. "You know, it was horrible," she said. "I felt discomfort. I didn't enjoy that experience!"

She said she loved me; it was the first time she had verbalized this freely and openly. She explained that if she knew that I loved her in return as she wanted her father to do, she could imagine leaving me. After this session she visited her lesbian friend briefly. As she drove home she thought of vermin in her genitalia, but was able to put the thought out of her mind and to analyze why she had gone to see the woman after the session in which she professed love for me. She realized that mature heterosexual love still frightened her with the possibility of disappointment and failure. Thus she had briefly regressed to the mother (the lesbian) to defend against her adult heterosexuality. I noted with pleasure her capacity for self-analysis.

She told me that something else had changed in her—she no longer blamed her parents for everything. She bought valentine cards for them, the first such cards she had given since she was in the eighth grade.

Return to Splitting

Pattie's visiting her split images, "the big bad blob," and the femme fatale, started when she saw a film about a woman with a split personality working by day in an office and plying her trade as a streetwalker by night. Fascinated, Pattie rented a videotape of the film and watched it three times in one day. "I am not alone in the world. Others also are attempting to merge opposite things in themselves," she said. In the film a man's love helps the heroine to mend her personality's split and to become a sexual woman without being a prostitute. But before her "cure" she kills a fanatical, harsh preacher who also lusted after her. He represented for Pattie the oedipal father and her harsh superego.

Associating with this, Pattie realized that she had unconsciously felt that it was her blossoming femininity when she was 8 that had depressed her father, just as the heroine of the film made the preacher crazy. She now recalled that her worst fear during the initial years of her treatment was boring me (making me depressed).

I pointed out that nothing she did changed her father's depression, and she unconsciously kept feeling responsible. Then she suggested that when we separated I might be sad and not be able to handle it. For a long time, the idea of this kept her from wanting to get well (blossom). I told her it was possible that I would feel sad when we separated, and that she would feel the same. I asked if she could tolerate such feelings without turning them into depression.

In the next session she continued to review her illness, her treatment, and the "last secrets." She was trying hard to see me as outside her transference neurosis.

She recalled having moved to the farm about eight years previously. She could stay with horses for a long time because they were not human and it was less hurtful to relate to them. She recalled how at that time she had found small tasks extremely onerous. For example, if she dropped a key, the effort of finding it was blown out of all proportion. "I am no longer frustrated with little things," she said.

THE ANALYST AS A NEW OBJECT

Pattie wanted to know how I manage my life. I was an analyst, the medical director of a general hospital, and she thought I traveled a good deal to give lectures. She asked how I delegated work to others; this was something that her father did not do easily.

She wondered about my family. She knew I had children. Once she had thought of my wife as a Barbie doll, but did so no longer. This had transference implications that required review. In her childhood bargain with her mother, the doll for which she had given up her pacifier had been a Barbie doll. Now she was surrendering the magic in her last such object—the pillow—voluntarily. I no longer had to own a Barbie doll. Instead of confiding details of my life outside my sessions with her, I told her that since she had been seeing me for years she did know much about me, and that while she might have some interest in knowing what my house looked like and so on, what was important was her knowing me through our verbal and nonverbal communication in our sessions. I told her that if she searched her mind she would find that she knew more about me than she thought, and she admitted that this was true.

GIVING UP THE PENIS

As we started her last month in treatment she came to a session with one foot bandaged and said that she had had a plantar wart removed. She had been told that the wart contained a virus. It was large, and when it had been excised by a laser she thought it resembled a snail in a shell, or a conch. She asked to take it home, and did so, keeping it on her dressing table. That night she dreamt of a famous male singer she doted on, who had, in fact, been a patient at the hospital in which she herself had been treated. In the dream she went with him to a fortress-like house with a broken gate surrounded by vines and bushes. While they were in the house the man took her vaginal secretion, put it in a test tube, and examined it, saying that it was not cancerous. This activity was carried out as though sexual relations were taking place, but it was "too clinical." Her associations revealed that the removal of the wart, which she described as "making a hole in my body," stood for her attempt to give up her penis. She had made such attempts in the past as she progressed in treatment. What was different now was her ready acceptance of her desire to have a penis and her ability to look *without* anxiety at the conflict between surrendering and not surrendering it. Moreover, she now showed real excitement at symbolically feminizing herself, reflecting where she was in this phase of her life. The gate surrounded by underbrush in her dream was her vagina; now it was opened. The hole in her body and the shell (a beautiful conch) represented the female genitalia. She was not yet sure how "well" her vagina was, but it was being treated "clinically."

The next day she noticed that the "snail" on her dressing table had shrunk, and in the afternoon it was gone. Apparently someone, probably her mother, who was at the farm at the time, had thrown it away while dusting. For a day or so she entertained the notion that it might reappear. It amused her to think that her unconscious processes made it hard for her to bid goodbye to her penis. She spoke of having had in the past a "prick-like personality," but said she was different now, more tactful and feminine. She gave me an example of how she had acted nicely in a social situation "maybe because I had my wart removed."

At the end of one session she "forgot" her purse, leaving it on the couch. I called this to her attention, adding that she was symbolically leaving her vagina behind for my "clinical" examination. I suggested that she herself would know if her vagina were functional.

REVIEWING THE PATHOGENIC TRAUMA

At her next session, hearing a small airplane overhead, Pattie fancied that it carried a banner advertising "Pattie's Sex Appeal." She continued the saga of her "battle wound" (the removal of the wart) for the next few weeks. Her foot hurt, and since she worked in a stable and was thus exposed to infection, her physician prescribed antibiotics and some painkiller that made her sleepy on the couch and induced a trance-like state. I could not determine whether her withdrawn appearance was entirely due to therapeutic regression, but in any case, the symbolism attached to the wounded foot now changed: Her mind and her associations to the bandage on her foot now related to her visiting her dominant pathogenic trauma—her mother's emphasis on caring for Mary and her orthopedic difficulty. Through her identification with the young Mary, and by examining this identification she was separating herself from the childhood environment she had experienced as noxious. Without any suggestion from me she tried to talk to her mother about how the latter recalled the childhood of the two sisters. Her mother was now able to recall—and confess to Pattie—that she had felt guilt over Mary's rotated hips; she spoke of having learned that this could be corrected, but of her distress over seeing Mary obliged to wear a brace.

Again, the Magical Pillow

Recalling that her mother collected bibelots, including figurines, she wondered if they represented Mary in her mother's mind. She also wondered whether her keeping the plastic bottle and her own habit of collecting things came from her identification with her mother. Then she returned to the pillow, another inanimate object with magical properties. She expressed appreciation for my having analyzed the meaning of the pillow instead of simply accepting it as a gift, which "would have belittled our relationship—made our relationship less." She was greatly saddened by our impending separation.

REVIEWING THE EXTERNAL REALITY

Three weeks before we were to terminate I changed the hour of Pattie's appointment with me. She "misunderstood" the hour and came to her session early. When she did not find me in the usual place, she walked up to the office in the main hospital where her treatment had started. I happened to be there and understood her mistake about the time to be due to her wish to return to the place where our relationship had begun—to say goodbye to it. She was pleased when I agreed to have our session in that office and recalled its appearance in the past. "There was a copper vase over there, and over there a jade tree." Her memory was accurate, although when we worked there the chaotic state of her mind did not allow her to perceive the reality of the room. She dreamt that night of being in her old neighborhood "having fun as a kid."

She was seeing one of her former lovers, who worked at the farm from time to time. She liked him, but not as a lover, and kept the relationship platonic, going with him as a friend to the movies and other places. Steve still worked on the farm, and when she was asked at a social gathering whether she knew him, she found herself saying proudly "Oh, yes. He works for me." She was the boss.

She came to an agreement with her father about her share of the profits of their horse operation. The farm manager and his wife still occupied a house on the farm, and her father now gave him notice to report to Pattie. "After my wart was cut off, my father respects me more!" she said jokingly. I noted that she was identifying with her perception of me as manager of a hospital.

Grieving after Termination

As termination approached she still expressed the wish to have a steady boyfriend and a loving relationship with a man before leaving treatment. She wanted to get married but wished to loosen her attachment to me before she could find a loving man. I helped her understand that she might continue grieving for months over separating from me, and I suggested that she be aware of this.

REVIEWING THE PATHOGENIC FANTASY

In the final week of her treatment, Pattie recaptured for the last time her dominant pathogenic fantasy. She had a dream and analyzed it with humor. One day after her session she asked to use my telephone to make a collect long-distance call. Since there are no other telephones in the building except in the three offices of faculty members, I agreed since I was about to leave anyway. This was an unusual request, but she seemed to feel some urgency about making the call. She said later that as she used the telephone she noticed a pair of scissors in a holder next to the instrument, and this contributed the day residue of a long dream she would have in which at first she was a princess in a big mansion which was invaded by strangers who partied loudly, and, in a sense, pushed her out. With the help of a man, she went back to what had been the mansion but was now but a modest, solidly built stone house. There she encountered a woman with scissors in her hand who tried to cut Pattie's hair. The scissors were sharp at first but became blunt. Pattie said that this dream was a review of her treatment: It indicated her wish to be her father's princess, as well as the presence of hidden grandiosity at the time she began treatment. The invaders of the house were her siblings. I had helped her return to the house and modify it. The woman with the scissors was the mother who used to cut Pattie's hair when she was small, hurting her as she cut it. (Her mother had also used scissors to cut her pacifier to bits.) This was a form of punishment that was eventually blunted.

During our discussion of what this punishment was, Pattie began to laugh. She had just realized the deeper wish contained in the dream. Her telephone call from my office had been to Mary, and Pattie found herself telling her sister that she was *alone* in her analyst's office and was using his telephone. It was then that she had noticed the scissors. In her dream, the woman with scissors also represented her aggressive self; she wanted to thrust the scissors into her mother's womb to kill Mary. When she told Mary that she was in her analyst's room alone she was expressing her wish to be the mother's/analyst's only child, after murdering Mary and the other siblings. The cutting of her hair and pacifier was her punishment for her murderous rage. This was an old story to her now, and instead of taking it as seriously as in the past, and with terror, she now could be not only amazed but amused by it.

LAST MOURNING AND CELEBRATION

Pattie's parents took her to dinner the day before we terminated, and they celebrated "her graduation," as she put it. She thanked them for having helped her financially with her treatment, toasted them, and told them that her work with me had made her "wiser, smarter, and able to deal with life better than most people in the world." Her parents in turn told her how pleased they were with her progress.

She wore a *black* shirt to her last appointment by way of mourning. On the couch she reported her last dream, about a white stucco house, which represented her analyzed self-representation. The house had "nice grass around it, and a pond, too. It had many, many beautiful arches" (representations of her feminine body). "There were horses near the house, and I fed them." She felt happy when she awakened and recalled this dream. "I expected to be very sad today," she said. "But I cried yesterday. It was O.K. to cry. I felt cleansed. Now I feel better because of it. I have no self-pity and no frustration."

During her last session she decided to get up off the couch and face me. She was rather shy and talked humorously of seeing many horses in her last dream. "I started with them; I am finishing with them," she mused.

She said she had wanted to wear a grey outfit for her last session, symbolizing the statement I had made long ago (see Step Two) about how the melding of black and white (her opposing object and self-representations) made grey. Then she thought it was more important to symbolize her mourning since it was her dominant feeling at the time. So she chose to wear black.

She said there was still much that she wanted to achieve. She was excited over being on her own, but anxious also. I recited a Turkish proverb: "When you see the village you are looking for, you do not need a guide any longer." She smiled, and as she left the room she gave me a brief hug.

Appendix

Some Guidelines for the Six-Step Program

Rather than trying to summarize all the issues addressed in this book, I will highlight some of its main conclusions.

Patients. I see persons with borderline personality organization on a spectrum, some being more disrupted than others. I have dealt in this book mainly with *psychosis-prone patients* who can be treated intensively for the resolution of their object relations conflicts and structural conflicts. The therapeutic frame of references is psychoanalytic.

Therapists. Therapists must have the ability *to regress in the service of the other* since they should meet their patients at their regressive states. They also should be capable of *therapeutic involvement in their patients' introjective-projective relatedness* so the patients can assimilate their useful functions such as analyzing and integrating. Such identification promotes the patients' progressive development. Systematic education and supervision of any therapist undertaking such therapeutic work is strongly recommended.

Treatment. *Treatment includes therapeutic regression in already regressed and/or undeveloped patients.* Such regression occurs after preparatory work and is followed by progressive development. The assumption is that under such circumstances patients have a better opportunity for structural changes that will last and make for healthier functioning.

Object relations conflicts vs. structural conflicts. Object relations conflicts dominate at first, although *object relations conflicts and structural conflicts may co-exist.* Object relations conflicts are dealt with first, perhaps requiring several years, before real work on the structural conflict begins. In fact, some or even most structural conflicts appear only after object relations conflicts are resolved and after the patient has developed more ability to repress.

Development in the "sophistication" of conflicts, and utilization of defenses dealing with such conflicts, can be seen throughout the whole treatment, although attention should be given to object relations conflicts, which return for a final review during the termination phase.

Generational continuity. Formed representations of others can be passed on to children from one generation to the next, and this sometimes leads to *opposing identifications in the developing psychic structure.* Therapists should be alert to this possibility.

Identification with the therapist's functions. One of the major curative factors in the treatment of the severely regressed and/or undeveloped patient is *the patient's identification with the therapist's functions.* The patient's identification with different functions of the therapist is sought at different steps of treatment. An adult patient, one who as a child did not have in his mothering person a source of certain functions useful for his development, may unconsciously receive such missing functions from his therapist.

The therapeutic alliance. The first and most important step is *to establish a core of the therapeutic alliance and to protect and maintain it.* When this is bypassed, the therapist's tools are useless.

Interpretations. Genetic aspects of the patient's conflicts are not initially interpreted. The severely regressed and/or undeveloped borderline patient may hear and understand such interpretations, but he lacks the ability to assimilate and use them. Here-and-now reflections of genetic conflicts are clarified, and *linking interpretations are offered to make the patient more "psychologically minded."*

Genetic interpretations are offered after the patient has experienced therapeutic regression followed by progressive development. However, the technique offered here emphasizes that before the patient comes to termination phase, he will uncover the unconscious aspects of the beginnings of his conflicts and reconstruct his infantile pathogenic fantasies.

Interpretations should be made to such patients from the side of the ego, with explanation of why the patient feels as he does, and how different thoughts are linked. For example, the therapist might say, "You may be angry because . . . " and then offer a connection between thought a and thought b. A stalemate may develop if the therapist habitually approaches his patient with interpretations from the side of the id or superego, saying, for example, without explanation, "You are angry" or "You punish yourself."

Limit setting. If from the outset the therapist sets limits for the purpose of protecting the therapeutic setting, the need for later, dramatic, limit setting will be reduced.

Stock taking. The severely regressed and/or undeveloped patient induces counterresponses in his therapist and there may be confusion at times as to what is taking place. *Consultation with one's own therapy notes and even consultation with colleagues* *should be considered.* Obviously, what is most important is empathic involvement with the patient within the sessions, but *thinking about the therapeutic process and stock taking outside sessions may guide the therapist.*

Transference psychosis. The six steps suggested in this book help with the management of a *transference psychosis.* It usually includes a "therapeutic story" during the evolution of which the patient moves out of his transference psychosis by using a newly created transitional object or phenomenon.

Transference neurosis. The "upward evolving" transference develops. The technique offered here refers to serious work with a *transference neurosis* once it develops.

Dream interpretations. *Dreams are initially interpreted according to the principle of so-called linking interpretations.* A link between the manifest content and day residue is found. Toward the end of the second step, the therapist begins to help his patient explore his dreams in order to understand the genetic input into his psychic development. From this phase onward, dream interpretation is an excellent way to help the patient connect here-and-now material with genetic material. During Steps Four, Five, and Six, dreams are interpreted as one interprets them to a neurotic patient.

The termination phase. The termination phase is particularly crucial for the patient who embarked on treatment as a severely regressed and/or undeveloped psychosis-prone borderline person. *The termination phase must be long enough to tie neatly all loose ends,* because if this is not done, the door stands open for future pathological regression under stressful conditions. With these patients the termination phase is actually like the classical psychoanalytical process. However, the therapist must be on guard against the patient's tendency to (re)use a hidden magical way of controlling separation from him, and for this purpose a gift might be offered. This should be analyzed.

The reward. Although intensive psychoanalytic psychotherapy of psychosis-prone borderline patients is taxing and time consuming, it is highly rewarding for the therapist. The experience becomes very personal and intimate, and the successful treatment of patients such as Pattie is not unlike the feeling of watching one's own child individuate and grow.

References

Abend, S. M., Porder, M. S., and Willick, M. S. (1983). *Borderline Patients: Psychoanalytic Perspectives.* New York: International Universities Press.

Abse, D. W., and Ewing, J. A. (1960). Some problems in psychotherapy with schizophrenic patients. *American Journal of Psychotherapy* 14:505–519.

Akhtar, S. (1984). The syndrome of identity diffusion. *American Journal of Psychiatry* 141:1381–1385.

Akhtar, S., and Thomson, J. A. (1982). Overview: narcissistic personality disorder. *American Journal of Psychiatry* 139:12–20.

Berg, M. D. (1977). The externalizing transference. *International Journal of Psycho-Analysis* 58:235–244.

Berkowitz, D. A., Shapiro, R. L., Zinner, J., and Shapiro, E. R. (1974). Concurrent family treatment of narcissistic disorders in adolescence. *International Journal of Psychoanalytic Psychotherapy* 3:379–396.

Berman, L. E. A. (1978). Sibling loss as an organizer of unconscious guilt: a case study. *Psychoanalytic Quarterly* 47:568–587.

Bird, B. (1972). Notes on transference: universal phenomenon and hardest part of analysis. *Journal of the American Psychoanalytic Association* 20:267–301.

Blos, P. (1968). Character formation in adolescence. In *The Adolescent Passage,* pp. 171–191. New York: International Universities Press, 1979.

Boyer, L. B. (1961). Provisional evaluation of psycho-analysis with few parameters in the treatment of schizophrenia. *International Journal of Psycho-Analysis* 42:389–403.

_____ (1967). Office treatment of schizophrenic patients: the use of psychoanalytic therapy with few parameters. In *Psychoanalytic Treatment of Characterological and Schizophrenic Disorders,* ed. L. B. Boyer and P. L. Giovacchini, pp. 143–188. New York: Science House.

_____ (1971). Psychoanalytic technique in the treatment of certain characterological and schizophrenic disorders. *International Journal of Psycho-Analysis* 52:67–86.

_____ (1977). Working with a borderline patient. In *Countertransference: The Therapist's Contribution to the Therapeutic Situation,* ed. L. Epstein and A. H. Feiner, pp. 533–574. New York: Jason Aronson.

_____ (1983). *The Regressed Patient.* New York: Jason Aronson.

_____ (1985). Discussion of "therapeutic regression and progressive development in the already severely regressed or undeveloped patient" by V. D. Volkan. Symposium on "intensive psychotherapy with disturbed people: fact or fiction." Children's Hospital, San Francisco, California, October 13.

_____ (1986). Technical aspects of treating the regressed patient. *Contemporary Psychoanalysis* 22:25–44.

Buie, D. H. (1985). Review of *Borderline Patients: Psychoanalytic Perspectives* by S. M. Abend, M. Porder, and M. S. Willick. *International Journal of Psycho-Analysis* 66:375–379.

Burnham, D. L. (1969). Schizophrenia and object relations. In *Schizophrenia and the Need-Fear Dilemma,* ed. D. L. Burnham, A. I. Gladstone, and R. W. Gibson, pp. 15–41. New York: International Universities Press.

Cain, A. C., and Cain, B. S. (1964). On replacing a child. *Journal of the American Academy of Child Psychiatry* 3:443–456.

Cambor, C. G. (1969). Preoedipal factors in superego development: the influence of multiple mothers. *Psychoanalytic Quarterly* 38:81–96.

Cameron, N. (1961). Introjection, reprojection, and hallucination in the interaction between schizophrenic patient and therapist. *International Journal of Psycho-Analysis* 42:86–96.

Coppolillo, H. P. (1967). Maturational aspects of the transitional phenomenon. *International Journal of Psycho-Analysis* 48:237–246.

Deutsch, H. (1942). Some forms of emotional disturbance and their relationship to schizophrenia. *Psychoanalytic Quarterly* 11:301–321.

Dewald, P.A. (1972). *The Psychoanalytic Process: A Case Illustration.* New York: Basic Books.

Dorpat, T. L. (1976). Structural conflict and object relations conflict. *Journal of the American Psychoanalytic Association* 24:855–874.

Elbirlik, K. (1980). Organ loss, grieving and itching. *American Journal of Psychotherapy* 84:523–533.

Erikson, E. H. (1950). Growth and crises of the healthy personality. In *Identity and the Life Cycle*, pp. 50–100. New York: International Universities Press.

_____ (1956). The problem of ego identity. *Journal of the American Psychoanalytic Association* 4:56–121.

Ferenczi, S. (1923). The dream of the "clever baby." In *Further Contributions to the Theory and Technique of Psycho-Analysis,* pp. 349–350. London: Hogarth Press, 1950.

_____ (1933). Confusion of tongues between adults and the child. In *Final Contributions to the Problems and Methods of Psycho-Analysis,* pp. 156–167. New York: Basic Books, 1955.

Fintzy, R. T. (1971). Vicissitudes of the transitional object in a borderline child. *International Journal of Psycho-Analysis* 52:107–114.

Freud, A. (1954). The widening scope of indications for psychoanalysis. In *The Writings of Anna Freud*, vol. 4, pp. 356–376. New York: International Universities Press, 1968.

_____ (1954b). Discussion remarks: problems of infantile neurosis. *The Psychoanalytic Study of the Child,* 9:71.

_____ (1963). The concept of developmental lines. *The Psychoanalytic Study of the Child* 18:245–265.

_____ (1965). Normality and pathology in childhood. In *The Writings of Anna Freud*, vol. 6. New York: International Universities Press, 1968.

Freud, S. (1937). Analysis terminable and interminable. *Standard Edition,* 23:216–253.

Fromm-Reichmann, F. (1950). *Principles of Intensive Psychotherapy.* Chicago: University of Chicago Press.

Frosch, J. (1970). Psychoanalytic considerations of the psychotic character. *Journal of the American Psychoanalytic Association* 18:24–50.

Gedo, J. E., and Goldberg, A. (1973). *Models of the Mind: A Psychoanalytic Theory*. Chicago: University of Chicago Press.

Giovacchini, P. L. (1967). Frustration and externalization. *Psychoanalytic Quarterly* 36:571–583.

_____ (1969). The influence of interpretation upon schizophrenic patients. *International Journal of Psycho-Analysis* 50:179–186.

_____ (1972). Interpretation and definition of the analytic setting. In *Tactics and Technique in Psychoanalytic Therapy,* ed. P. L. Giovacchini, pp. 291–304. New York: Science House.

_____ (1975). Various aspects of the analytic process. In *Tactics and Techniques in Psychoanalytic Therapy,* vol. II, ed. P. L. Giovacchini, pp. 5–94. New York: Jason Aronson.

_____ (1979). *Treatment of Primitive Mental States*. New York: Jason Aronson.

_____ (1986). *Developmental Disorders: The Transitional Space in Mental Breakdown and Creative Integration*. New York: Jason Aronson.

Glover, E. (1955). *Technique of Psychoanalysis*. New York: International Universities Press.

Green, N., and Solnit, A. J. (1964). Reactions to a threatened loss of a child: a vulnerable child syndrome. *Pediatrics* 34:58–66.

Greenacre, P. (1970). The transitional object and the fetish: with special reference to the role of illusion. *International Journal of Psychoanalysis* 51:447–456.

_____ (1975). On reconstruction. *Journal of the American Psychoanalytic Association* 23:693–712.

Greenson, R. (1958). On screen defenses, screen hunger, and screen identity. In *Explorations in Psychoanalysis,* pp. 111–132. New York: International Universities Press, 1978.

_____ (1966). That "impossible" profession. *Journal of the American Psychoanalytic Association* 14:9–27.

Greenspan, S. I. (1977). The oedipal-preoedipal dilemma. *International Review of Psycho-Analysis* 4:381–391.

Grinberg, L. (1979). Countertransference and counteridentification. *Contemporary Psychoanalysis* 15:226–247.

Gunderson, J. T. (1977). Characteristics of borderlines. In *Borderline Personality Disorders: The Concept, the Syndrome, the Patient,* pp. 173–192. New York: International Universities Press.

Gunderson, J. T., Carpenter, W. T., and Strauss, J. S. (1975). Borderline and schizophrenic patients: a comparative study. *American Journal of Psychiatry* 132:1259–1264.

Hann-Kende, F. (1933). On the role of transference and countertransference in psychoanalysis. In *Psychoanalysis and the Occult*, ed. G. Devereux, pp. 158–167. New York: International Universities Press, 1953.

Hendrick, I. (1951). Early development of the ego: identification in infancy. *Psychoanalytic Quarterly* 20:44–61.

Hurn, H. T. (1970). Adolescent transference: a problem of the terminal phase of analysis. *Journal of the American Psychoanalytic Association* 18:342–357.

Jacobson, E. (1964). *The Self and the Object World.* New York: International Universities Press.

Kafka, J. S. (1969). The body as transitional object: a psychoanalytic study of a self-mutilating patient. *British Journal of Medical Psychology* 43:207–212.

Kahne, N. (1967). On the persistence of transitional phenomena into adult life. *International Journal of Psycho-Analysis* 48:247–258.

Kavanaugh, J. G., and Volkan, V. D. (1978). Transsexualism and a new type of psychosurgery: thoughts on MacVicar's paper. *International Journal of Psychoanalytic Psychotherapy* 7:366–372.

Kernberg, O. F. (1965). Notes on countertransference. *Journal of the American Psychoanalytic Association* 13:38–56.

_____ (1967). Borderline personality organization. *Journal of the American Psychoanalytic Association* 15:641–685.

_____ (1970). A psychoanalytic classification of character pathology. *Journal of the American Psychoanalytic Association* 18:800–822.

_____ (1975). *Borderline Conditions and Pathological Narcissism.* New York: Jason Aronson.

_____ (1976a). Foreword to *Primitive Internalized Object Relations,* by V. D. Volkan. New York: International Universities Press.

_____ (1976b). *Object Relations Theory and Clinical Psychoanalysis.* New York: Jason Aronson.

_____ (1980). *Internal World and External Reality.* New York: Jason Aronson.

_____ (1984). *Severe Personality Disorders: Psychotherapeutic Strategies.* New Haven: Yale University Press.

Khan, M. M. R. (1974). *The Privacy of the Self: Papers on Psychoanalytic Theory and Technique.* New York: International Universities Press.

Klein, M. (1946). Notes on some schizoid mechanisms. *International Journal of Psycho-Analysis* 27:99–110.

_____ (1955). On identification. In *Directions in Psychoanalysis,* ed. M. Klein, P. Heimann, and R. E. Money-Kyrle, pp. 309–345. London: Tavistock.

Knight, R. (1953). Borderline states. *Bulletin of the Menninger Clinic* 17:1–12.

Kohut, H. (1971). *The Analysis of the Self.* New York: International Universities Press.

Kramer, P. (1955). On discovering one's identity. *The Psychoanalytic Study of the Child* 10:47–74.

Kramer, S. (1986). Identification and its vicissitudes as observed in children: a developmental approach. *International Journal of Psycho-Analysis* 67:161–172.

Kubie, L. S. (1968). Unsolved problems in the resolution of the transference. *Psychoanalytic Quarterly* 37:331–352.

Langs, R., and Searles, H. F. (1980). *Intrapsychic and Interpersonal Dimensions of Treatment.* New York: Jason Aronson.

Lerner, H. D., and Lerner, P. M. (1982). A comparative study of defensive structure in neurotic, borderline, and schizophrenic patients. *Psychoanalysis and Contemporary Thought* 5:77–115.

Lerner, H. D., Sugarman, A., and Gaughran, J. (1981). Borderline and schizophrenic patients: a comparative study of defensive structure. *Journal of Nervous and Mental Disorders* 169:705–711.

Lindon, J. A., ed. (1967). On regression: a workshop. *Psychoanalytic Forum* 2:293–316.

Little, M. I. (1981). *Transference Neurosis and Transference Psychosis.* New York: Jason Aronson.

Loewald, H. W. (1960). On the therapeutic action of psychoanalysis. *International Journal of Psycho-Analysis* 41:16–33.

_____ (1982). Regression: some general considerations. In *Technical Factors in the Treatment of the Severely Disturbed Patient,* ed. P. L. Giovacchini, and L. B. Boyer, pp. 107–130. New York: Jason Aronson.

Mack, J. E. (1984). Paper presented at the Committee on International Relations at the Fall Meeting of the Group for the Advancement of Psychiatry (GAP), November 10–12.

Mahler, M. S. (1963). Thoughts about development and individuation. *The Psychoanalytic Study of the Child* 18:307–324. New York: International Universities Press.

_____ (1968). *On Human Symbiosis and the Vicissitudes of Individuation.* New York: International Universities Press.

_____ (1972). A study of the separation–individuation process and its possible application to borderline phenomena in the psychoanalytic situation. *The Psychoanalytic Study of the Child* 27:403–424.

Meissner, W. (1978). Theoretical assumptions of concepts of the borderline personality. *Journal of the American Psychoanalytic Association* 26:557–595.

Miller, I. (1965). On the return of symptoms in the terminal phase of psychoanalysis. *International Journal of Psycho-Analysis* 45:487–501.

Modell, A. H. (1963). Primitive object relationships and the predisposition to schizophrenia. *International Journal of Psycho-Analysis* 44:282–292.

_____ (1968). *Object Love and Reality*. New York: International Universities Press.

_____ (1976). The "holding environment" and the therapeutic action of psychoanalysis. *Journal of the American Psychoanalytic Association* 24:285–307.

Niederland, W. G. (1956). Clinical observations on the "little man" phenomenon. *The Psychoanalytic Study of the Child* 11:381–395.

Novey, S. (1968). *The Second Look: The Reconstruction of Personal History in Psychiatry and Psychoanalysis.* Baltimore: Johns Hopkins University Press.

Novick, J. (1982). Termination. *Psychoanalytic Inquiry* 2:329–365.

Novick, J., and Kelly, K. (1970). Projection and externalization. *The Psychoanalytic Study of the Child* 25:69–95.

Olinick, S. L. (1964). The negative therapeutic reaction. *International Journal of Psycho-Analysis* 45:540–548.

_____ (1969). Empathy and Regression. In *The Psychotherapeutic Instrument,* pp. 3–16. New York: Jason Aronson, 1980.

_____ (1970). Panel report: the negative therapeutic reaction. *Journal of the American Psychoanalytic Association* 18:655–672.

_____ (1980). *The Psychotherapeutic Instrument*. New York: Jason Aronson.

Olinick, S. L., Poland, W. S., Grigg, K. A., and Granatir, W. L. (1973). The psycho-analytic work ego: process and interpretaion. *International Journal of Psycho-Analysis* 54:143–151.

Ornstein, A., and Ornstein, P. H. (1975). On the interpretive process in schizophrenia. *International Journal of Psychoanalytic Psychotherapy* 4:219–271.

Özbek, A., and Volkan, V. D. (1976). Psychiatric problems within the satellite extended families of Turkey. *American Journal of Psychotherapy* 30:576–582.

Pao, P-N. (1965). The role of hatred in the ego. *Psychoanalytic Quarterly* 34:257–264.

_____ (1979). *Schizophrenic Disorders.* New York: International Universities Press.

Poznanski, E. O. (1972). The "replacement child": a saga of unresolved parental grief. *Behavioral Pediatrics* 81: 1190–1193.

Racker, H. (1968). *Transference and Countertransference.* New York: International Universities Press.

Rangell, L. (1966). An overview of the ending of an analysis. In *Psychoanalysis in the Americas,* ed. R.E. Litman, pp. 141–173. New York: International Universities Press.

_____ (1979). Countertransference issues in the theory of therapy. *Journal of the American Psychoanalytic Association* (Suppl.) 27:81–112.

Rapaport, D. (1952). Projective techniques and the theory of thinking. In *The Collected Papers of David Rapaport,* ed. M. M. Gill, pp. 461–469. New York: Basic Books, 1967.

Rosenfeld, H. A. (1954). Considerations regarding the psycho-analytic approach to acute and chronic schizophrenia. *International Journal of Psycho-Analysis* 35:135–140.

_____ (1966). Discussion of "office treatment of schizophrenic patients" by L. B. Boyer. *The Psychoanalytic Forum* 1:351–353.

Schowalter, J. E. (1983). Some meanings of being a horsewoman. *The Psychoanalytic Study of the Child* 38:501–517. New Haven: Yale University Press.

Schulz, C. G. (1980). The contribution of the concept of self-representation—object-representation differentiation to the understanding of the schizophrenias. In *The Course of Life: Psychoanalytic Contributions toward Understanding Personality Development.* Vol. III, ed. S. I. Greenspan, and G. H. Pollock, pp. 453–470. Washington, D.C.: NIMH.

Searles, H. F. (1963). Transference psychosis in the psychotherapy of chronic schizophrenia. *International Journal of Psycho-Analysis* 44:249–281.

_____ (1966). *Collected Papers on Schizophrenia and Related Subjects.* New York: International Universities Press.

_____ (1975). The patient as therapist to his analyst. In *Tactics and Techniques in Psychoanalytic Therapy Vol. II: Countertransference,* ed. D. L. Giovacchini, pp. 95–151. New York: Jason Aronson.

_____ (1976). Transitional phenomena and therapeutic symbiosis. *International Journal of Psychoanalytic Psychotherapy* 5:145–204.

_____ (1977). Dual- and multiple-identity processes in borderline ego functioning. In *Borderline Personality Disorders: The Concept, the Syndrome, the Patient,* pp. 441–455. New York: International Universities Press.

_____ (1978). Techniques of therapy. In *My Work with Borderline Patients,* pp. 3–25. New York: Jason Aronson.

_____ (1979). *Countertransference and Related Subjects.* New York: International Universities Press.

_____ (1982). Some aspects of separation and loss in psychoanalytic therapy with borderline patients. In *My Work with Borderline Patients,* pp. 287–326. New York: Jason Aronson, 1986.

_____ (1986). *My Work with Borderline Patients.* New York: Jason Aronson.

Shapiro, E. R., Shapiro, R. L., Zinner, J., and Berkowitz, D. A. (1977). The borderline ego and the working alliance. *International Journal of Psycho-Analysis* 58:77–87.

Shapiro, E. R., Zinner, J., Shapiro, R. L., and Berkowitz, D. A. (1975). The influence of family experience on borderline personality development. *International Review of Psycho-Analysis* 2:399–411.

Smith, L. (1949). *Killers of the Dream.* New York: W. W. Norton.

Socarides, C. W. (1978). *Homosexuality.* New York: Jason Aronson.

Spitz, R. A. (1957). *No and Yes: On the Beginning of Human Communication.* New York: International Universities Press.

Stone, M. H. (1980). *The Borderline Syndrome.* New York: McGraw-Hill.

Tähkä, V. (1979). Psychotherapy as phase-specific interaction: towards a general psychoanalytic theory of psychotherapy. *Scandinavian Psychoanalytic Review* 2:113–132.

_____ (1984). Psychoanalytic treatment as a developmental continuum: considerations of disturbed structuralization and its phase-specific encounter. *Scandinavian Psychoanalytic Review* 7:133–159.

Tähkä, V., Rechardt, E., and Achté, K. A. (1971). Psychoanalytic aspects of the Finnish sauna bath. *Psychiatrica Fennica* 63–72.

Ticho, E. E. (1972). Termination of psychoanalysis: treatment goals, life goals. *Psychoanalytic Quarterly* 41:315–333.

van der Waals, H. G. (1952). Discussion of the mutual influences in the development of ego and id. *The Psychoanalytic Study of the Child* 7:66–68. New York: International Universities Press.

Volkan, V. D. (1965). The observation of the "little man" phenomenon in a case of anorexia nervosa. *British Journal of Medical Psychology* 38:299–311.

_____ (1968). The introjection of and identification with the therapist as

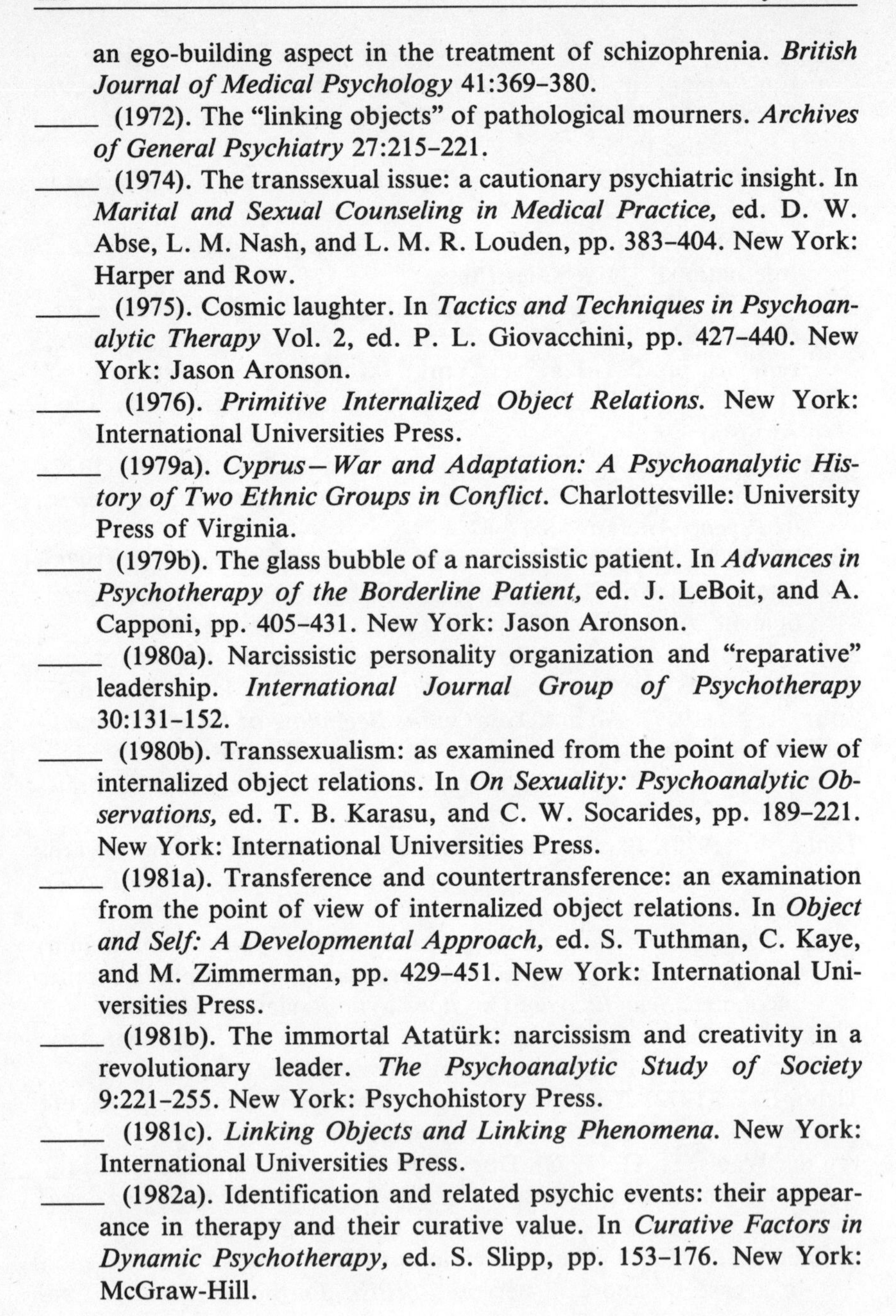

an ego-building aspect in the treatment of schizophrenia. *British Journal of Medical Psychology* 41:369–380.

_____ (1972). The "linking objects" of pathological mourners. *Archives of General Psychiatry* 27:215–221.

_____ (1974). The transsexual issue: a cautionary psychiatric insight. In *Marital and Sexual Counseling in Medical Practice,* ed. D. W. Abse, L. M. Nash, and L. M. R. Louden, pp. 383–404. New York: Harper and Row.

_____ (1975). Cosmic laughter. In *Tactics and Techniques in Psychoanalytic Therapy* Vol. 2, ed. P. L. Giovacchini, pp. 427–440. New York: Jason Aronson.

_____ (1976). *Primitive Internalized Object Relations.* New York: International Universities Press.

_____ (1979a). *Cyprus—War and Adaptation: A Psychoanalytic History of Two Ethnic Groups in Conflict.* Charlottesville: University Press of Virginia.

_____ (1979b). The glass bubble of a narcissistic patient. In *Advances in Psychotherapy of the Borderline Patient,* ed. J. LeBoit, and A. Capponi, pp. 405–431. New York: Jason Aronson.

_____ (1980a). Narcissistic personality organization and "reparative" leadership. *International Journal Group of Psychotherapy* 30:131–152.

_____ (1980b). Transsexualism: as examined from the point of view of internalized object relations. In *On Sexuality: Psychoanalytic Observations,* ed. T. B. Karasu, and C. W. Socarides, pp. 189–221. New York: International Universities Press.

_____ (1981a). Transference and countertransference: an examination from the point of view of internalized object relations. In *Object and Self: A Developmental Approach,* ed. S. Tuthman, C. Kaye, and M. Zimmerman, pp. 429–451. New York: International Universities Press.

_____ (1981b). The immortal Atatürk: narcissism and creativity in a revolutionary leader. *The Psychoanalytic Study of Society* 9:221–255. New York: Psychohistory Press.

_____ (1981c). *Linking Objects and Linking Phenomena.* New York: International Universities Press.

_____ (1982a). Identification and related psychic events: their appearance in therapy and their curative value. In *Curative Factors in Dynamic Psychotherapy,* ed. S. Slipp, pp. 153–176. New York: McGraw-Hill.

_____ (1982b). Narcissistic personality disorder. In *Critical Problems in Psychiatry*, ed. J. O. Cavenar, and H. K. Brodie, pp. 332–350. Philadelphia: Lippincott.

_____ (1982c). A young woman's inability to say no to needy people and her identification with the frustrator in the analytic situation. In *Technical Factors in the Treatment of the Severely Disturbed Patient,* ed. P. L.Giovacchini, and L. B. Boyer, pp. 439–465. New York: Jason Aronson.

_____ (1984). *What Do You Get when You Cross a Dandelion with a Rose? The True Story of a Psychoanalysis.* New York: Jason Aronson.

_____ (1985a). The need to have enemies and allies: a developmental approach. *Political Psychology* 2:219–247.

_____ (1985b). Suitable targets of externalization and schizophrenia. In *Towards a Comprehensive Model of Schizophrenic Disorders,* ed. D. B. Finesilver, pp. 125–153. New York: Analytic Press.

_____ (1985c). Becoming an analyst. In *Analysts at Work: Practice, Principles and Techniques,* ed. J. Reppen, pp. 215–231. New York: Analytic Press.

_____ (1986). The narcissism of minor differences in the psychological gap between opposing nations. *Psychoanalytic Inquiry* 6:175–191.

Volkan, V. D., and Akhtar, S. (1979). The symptoms of schizophrenia. In *Integrating Ego Psychology and Object Relations Theory,* ed. L. Saretsky, G. D. Goldman, and D. S. Milman, pp. 270–285. Dubuque, Iowa: Kendall/Hunt.

Volkan, V. D., and Berent, S. (1976). Psychiatric aspects of surgical treatment for problems of sexual identification (transsexualism). In *Modern Perspectives in the Psychiatric Aspects of Surgery,* ed. J. Howells, pp. 447–467. New York: Brunner-Mazel.

Volkan, V. D., and Cevik, A. (in press). Turkish fathers and their families. In *Fathers and Their Families,* ed. S. Cath, A. Gurwitt, and L. Grinberg. New York: International Universities Press.

Volkan, V. D., and Corney, R.T. (1968). Some considerations of satellite states and satellite dreams. *British Journal of Medical Psychology* 41:282–290.

Volkan, V. D., and Kavanaugh, J. G. (1978). The cat people. In *Between Fantasy and Reality: Transitional phenomena and objects,* ed. S. Grolnick, L. Barkin, and W. Muensterberger, pp. 289–303. New York: Jason Aronson.

Volkan, V. D., and Itzkowitz, N. (1984). *The Immortal Atatürk: A*

Psychobiography. Chicago: University of Chicago Press.

Wallerstein, R. S. (1986). *42 Lives in Treatment: A Study of Psychoanalysis and Psychotherapy*. New York: Guilford Press.

Weigert, E. (1952). Contribution to the problem of terminating psychoanalyses. *Psychoanalytic Quarterly* 21:465–480.

Winnicott, D. W. (1953). Transitional objects and transitional phenomena. *International Journal of Psycho-Analysis* 34:89–97.

____ (1956). On transference. *International Journal of Psycho-Analysis* 37:386–388.

____ (1960). The theory of the parent–infant relationship. In *The Maturational Processes and the Facilitating Environment,* pp. 37–55. New York: International Universities Press, 1965.

____ (1971). *Playing and Reality*. London: Tavistock.

Zetzel, E. R. (1971). A developmental approach to the borderline patient. *American Journal of Psychiatry* 127:867–871.

Zinner, J., and Shapiro, R. (1972). Projective identification as a mode of perception and behavior in families of adolescents. *International Journal of Psycho-Analysis* 53:527–530.

Zuckerman, R., and Volkan, V. D. (in press). Complicated mourning over a body defect: the making of a "living linking object." In *The Problem of Loss and Mourning: A Psychoanalytic Perspective,* ed. D. Deitrich and P. Shabad. New York: International Universities Press.

Index